Spanish Leaves

❧ ☙

Spanish Leaves

❧ ❧

Honor Tracy

LONDON
METHUEN & CO LTD
11 NEW FETTER LANE · EC4

To Robert Liddell

❧ I ❧

ONE YEAR I TOOK A COTTAGE WITH A GARDEN ON THE
coast of Andalusia and lived there for six months. In this way
I saw the country under a new aspect, which is not to say that
my vision of it was clearer or likely to be more true. While we
are travelling about things will occur which impress, attract
or move us in a particular and immediate way and we evaluate
them by the light of nature or of experience. When we stay
in one place the commentaries of people round us nibble at
the edges of our impressions and our own wider information
will often blur them.

Once as I strolled through Seville just before Holy Week
there was a man kneeling in the open street before the Christ
Crucified. He was old and dirty and ragged and appeared
unconscious of anything in the world but the figure hanging
above him: his arms were held out in imitation of it, the
emaciated hands seeming to beg for nails to pierce them. I
will not say that such things happen only in Spain but it is
only there that I have seen them, and the memory of this
instance has never faded through the years: as if it happened
only yesterday I remember the details of that scene, the man's
knobby cheek-bones with the skin taut over them and his
matted grey hair, the hollow eyes that reflected something of
the agony of the Passion, the humble adoration, the utter
abandonment of the self.

Had I not been going away that afternoon, had I been
established in Seville with a circle of acquaintance, it would
all have been different. I would have mentioned a scene which

7

had so moved me to somebody, with who knows what disturbing results. The disillusioning of visitors is a national sport and if there is one thing that apparently annoys the educated Andalusian more than criticism, it is praise. "Bless you!" my friend might have said. "That was old Pepe Moreno. The Turismo pays him to carry on like that when foreigners are about." Already a shadow would have fallen across the incident and confusion would slide into my ideas like an otter among fish. Inevitably, Turismo's malfeasance would have been referred to some other local sage and then, if I know anything about it, the reply would have been something like this: "Ah! You've been talking to Don Jacinto. Don't you know that he is Liberal and anti-clerical? He will say anything against religion. As a matter of fact, the man you saw is noble and extremely rich, but ever since his mother died in 1943 . . ." And so it would continue: it would be impossible to determine whether skin after skin of falsehood were being stripped like the coats of an onion from a core of truth or whether, on the contrary, veil after veil were being drawn across it. The one sure thing is that the memory of the kneeling man would never be clear and simple again.

That is just one side of it, and a negative side. In other ways the experience will be rewarding and often salutary. G. K. Chesterton once remarked that less French was needed to carry on a philosophical discussion than to buy a safety-pin and until we have checked over the inventory of a house we may have supposed that our vocabulary was adequate. *Atizadores* 2, *alforjas* 2, *mamparas* 3, *escobillas* 2. . . . There is not even a thread of sense to guide us, the lists of words have to be learned, we are back at school. We discover that keeping house in Spain is exactly like keeping house at home up to the moment when it is suddenly and explosively different, and the servants walk out. Many things become invisible through familiarity but others come forward in their place; and we enjoy that pleasantest of human conditions, which is to be part of something and a little separated at the same time.

The house was near Arroyo de la Miel, or Stream of Honey, a village about twelve miles south of Malaga at the foot of the hills. It stood with its garden inside a *finca* belonging to a business man from Malaga who cared a great deal about money. In fact he seemed to like it better than anything else. With the Spanish need always to make manifest, to display, wealthy Spaniards are apt to go in for diamond rings and shiny motor-cars and paunches, but Don Gabriel was satisfied merely to possess and to contemplate. He was the first Spaniard of this type I had encountered and his passion seemed more intense and purer than that of his like in other lands. Rents had always to be paid in advance and on the nail, and a delay of only a few hours would make him well-nigh delirious. He would probe minutely into its cause, trembling like a leaf meanwhile, and shoot out a flow of suggestions as to how it might be overcome. And he never would let the property for periods of less than three months together: he exacted the full amount, were it in actual use for only a week or ten days.

On this point there was a disagreement with the tenant who followed me, an American who stayed a while and then wanted to change to a monthly basis for greater freedom of movement. They argued and argued and neither would give way. Soon afterwards Don Gabriel fell dangerously ill and the kind American called at the clinic to see if there were anything he could do. "Yes," came the unhesitating reply: "pay three months' rent in advance." Then, smiling, Don Gabriel lay back on his pillows and shortly after expired.

When I was there, however, he still had eighteen months to go and he schemed and worried and calculated as if he were going to live for ever.

The house was kept by a maid from the village, called Purificación, who sang all day long in the drilling voice of a cat on the roof. She had a small repertoire of vocal works all concerned with *amor* and *sufrimiento* and *corazón* and she ran

9

through it tirelessly, always in the same order. When she had completed a cycle she began it again at once. I implored her not to sing when I was at work and she was nearly as amazed by that as by my being so odd a thing as a writer at all. The hideous row she made came as naturally to her as breathing did, and how anyone could object to it was beyond her powers of comprehension. Directly my chair went back at the end of the morning's stint the terrible sounds began again.

Men had a stupendous effect on the nubile Puri. If one appeared and I should call her to bring drinks, an interval would follow while she flew into the garden to pick a flower for her hair. Then she would bring the tray, blushing and smirking and throwing glances about, and finally, reluctantly, retire to the kitchen where she broke into song, on an entirely new note now, an eerie jungle mating-call that made the blood run cold. There was little need of a telephone in my *casita*. If something were needed from Arroyo, Puri threw up the window and screamed at the house above us, where someone closely resembling her would scream to the next and so on until it sounded as if the hillside were alive with peacocks.

I learned to housekeep in the Andalusian way, which is to buy only what will be used at the next meal. Experience taught me this, for anything bought in bulk was ruthlessly squandered and anything not eaten at once was never seen again. Good olive oil was not to be had at the lawful price that winter – a periodic affliction due to various corrupt practices – and with patience and cunning I managed to buy a drum on the black market of a size that should have lasted out my stay. It went faster than if I had drunk a pint of it with every meal. As for leftovers, three-quarters of a fat chicken, a string of *chorizos* (a delicious, very expensive kind of sausage) and nearly the whole of a *manchego* cheese, all disappeared in quick succession.

I would bear it no longer and asked Puri where the cheese had gone. She was ironing at the time and she hurled the iron across the room. She flew into a rage, a glorious Spanish rage, with eye-flashing, heel-stamping and finger-snapping, that ignited spontaneously and required no stoking at all. She shrieked that if the Señora did not trust her she had better go at once. No one had ever cast such a slur on her before in the whole of her life. She was poor but she was honest. . . .

"But where is the cheese?" I repeated, with insufferable calm.

"The cheese? The cheese?" the frivolous question merely goaded her anew. "I took it home." But the Señora was not going to get away with this. Don Gabriel should hear of it. The priest should hear of it. She was poor but she was honest. Her parents were poor and *they* were honest. . . .

"Why did you take it home?" I plodded on.

"Why? Why? Why?" Puri glared at me. "Was I to put it on the Señora's table? A cut cheese?" She would have her wages and she would go. She had always worked for Señoras. She was poor but . . .

In truth, I was never quite good enough for Puri. It was not only my vulgar way of finishing cheeses up, but also of doing things for myself. The reproach in her eyes when she caught me sewing on a button or carrying a log to the fire would pierce me to the heart. But there was vanity, not humility, behind it, for Puri was afraid the other maids would say her employer was not a real lady accustomed from birth to be waited on hand and foot.

If I had been a fixture in her village, she would undoubtedly have spoken her mind. The relationship between master and servant in Spain is different from ours and very charming. The Spaniard will work like a mule for his meagre wage and put up with long hours, discomfort and a total lack of consideration, but he never hesitates to reprove if he deems it called for. I used to carouse with a bibulous old gentleman in Madrid who would sit up till all hours with his cronies about him, roaring ever and anon for the ancient housekeeper to bring in wine. She never dreamed of disobeying or asking when she might go to bed, but came slowly and painfully, wheezing and groaning, with the jug in her hands and grumbled as she came: "Don Rafael! How many more? You have had far too much already. At your time of life! Are you a Christian? Do you not know how near is the end?" She said "Don Rafael" and "you" and he said "Maria" and "thou", but otherwise there was nothing in tone or word to indicate the smallest inequality. "Silence, thou!" he would chortle: "take thy long face out of here!" And if he spilt a drop of wine he roared for her to come and wipe the table, if he dropped his handkerchief she must hobble up from the kitchen again in order to retrieve it, scolding all the while. It was better than a play to watch them, and both found the arrangement perfectly natural and proper.

But I was only a bird of passage and, worse, a foreigner and Puri dealt patiently and courteously with me. I was always "La Señora" in spite of my *estado civil*, just as the man of the house is always "Señorito", even though a grandfather. I did many terrible things. I wrote books and lived alone, whereas I ought to have been dressed in black and beginning to think about some grandchildren. I smoked, which in the countryside only women of low repute indulged in. My celibacy troubled the poor girl more than anything else and she was fond of hinting that would I only bestir myself there might still be hope. Male visitors were received with a look of frank and eager surmise and afterwards I had to hear how charming they were and how obviously attached to the Señora.

There was really nothing at all in her little brain-box but the *novio*, a decent lad from the next village. I only spoke to him once, but he left a clear impression. Puri came bursting in while I was at work and said he was there at the door to see me. Her orders were never to interrupt me unless the matter were very important and as a rule she adhered to this, so faithfully indeed that when the house was burning once she fought the flames alone. It transpired that Paco had merely caught and caged a wild bird which he wanted to sell, and I was rather vexed. But Puri had her answer ready and it was a good, sufficient one. "It *was* very important, for him," she explained. Her eyes glowed like those of a cat in the dark when she spoke his name, and the days when he walked over the hill to see her were days of wreckage and madness. Twice during my stay in Arroyo there was a fiesta in a village somewhere near and Puri, chattering like an ape with excitement, borrowed on her wages and tricked herself out in all her finery. They had to walk a dozen miles or so, barefoot and carrying their good shoes in one hand, and then she danced and sang and laughed all night and only stumbled wearily into the house again as the sun came up over the sea.

An old beggar-woman came once a week to collect alms. She was a wizened old crone like a walking bundle of rags and her gnarled hands were always clenched as if gripping a broom or scythe. She had steady grey eyes and great natural dignity: for that matter, no people I ever knew understand the noble art of asking and receiving as well as the Spanish, and if anyone whines or wheedles in Spain, it is almost sure to be a gipsy. She came always on the day and at the hour she was asked to come and with the greatest composure began talking about the need for rain or the state of the crops or the catches of fish, in a good sharp Castilian that was refreshing after the slovenly Andaluz. Next she inquired after my health with an almost maternal solicitude: and only after a decent lapse of time would take her bread and oil and money, return thanks in the beautiful formula: *Dios se lo pague!*, and creep back to her ruined cottage on the hill. This ritual we never varied until the day I had to tell her that I was going home. Then she burst into a storm of weeping, kissing my hand and calling me *hijita*, and finally, slowly and painfully hobbled away, a little bowed figure that looked as if misery itself were wandering through the fields.

A charming man was the postman, rosy-cheeked, blue-eyed and smiling, who arrived on a gleaming scarlet motor-bicycle soon after lunch. When there were fat important foreign letters

13

he hooted gaily as he turned in at the drive and when there was just a bill or a newspaper he handed it to me apologetically, shrugging his shoulders as if he were in some way to blame. About the third or fourth visit he coughed in a warning manner and with a grave expression remarked that he was under no moral or legal *obligación* to deliver my letters at all. I meditated this piece of information, wondering what a postman's *obligaciones* could conceivably consist of, if not of that. It was not the first time that this unusual point of view had cropped up. Once before I had spent some months together in Spain, living at the top of a rather steep hill and as the days went by could not but notice that no one apparently was writing to me. Below in the village the postman could be seen wending his way with diligence from door to door, but he never turned up the steep rocky path that led to my house. At last I went down to inquire at the Post Office and he bounded across the village square to intercept me. "I was about to visit you," he cried. "These came in to-day." And he handed me an armful of letters, anything up to a month old.

The meaning of the Arroyo postman was clear enough and I promised that if he would bring the letters he should not lose by it. I would have tipped him monthly in any case, for in Spain an astonishing number and variety of people have to be tipped, postmen, policemen, shop assistants, civil servants and, for all I know, the executioner. It relieved the postman to find the new tenant of the little house a responsible human being and thereafter he took the greatest interest in my affairs. Like so many of his people, while he might be negligent of his own duties he was always prepared to help in matters that did not really concern him. Once he rode the whole way from Torremolinos with ice because I was going to give a party and the ice-man had not come, and once he killed a snake that was frightening Puri and me out of our wits.

All through the winter lunch was laid on the sunny terrace, above a bed of sweet violets, with the clear blue sea just beyond the boundary of the *finca*. Small green lizards streaked over rocks and trees or froze in their acrobatic postures while taking me in with eyes of sparkling gold. Antonio the old gardener moved stiffly about with his old straw hat pulled over his eyes, his jaw and chin like carved mahogany. One of his chores was to pump water into the *pozo* or tank and the *pozo* had a leak, although no one knew of this until long afterwards. I constantly sent word for the pump to be started and Antonio would throw down the tool in his hand with a kind of dull despair and start for the pump room, muttering comminations as he went. His own use of water both inside and out was of the most sparing, and he plainly thought me little better than a buffalo.

Every afternoon after lunch, punctual and discreet and reserved as the old beggar herself, Sultan came. He was a big yellow dog like an under-sized lion and his ears had been cropped to the roots, a wicked thing that is often done by Spanish peasants who believe it makes the animal fierce and so a better watch-dog. Sultan came straight to the kitchen door and waited there in silence looking through it with melancholy brown eyes. He took pot-luck with philosophy, whether it was bread or meat or *cocido* or rice. One day he came with a hungry little puppy trotting on either side of him, with an avuncular air as if he were saying, "Come along, children. I know a foreigner." He belonged to a family living higher up the hill who also possessed a thin pig, a thin mule and a fig tree without any figs. When they saw how the land lay they stopped feeding Sultan altogether. In the five months I knew him his expression and demeanour never altered once: he was always sullen and sad, yet resigned and pacific. He never wagged his tail when food was brought and any remarks addressed to him he ignored; and if I ever tried to stroke him his fur rose and his brow wrinkled and he backed away, grumbling under his breath. Whatever the human race had done to Sultan was beyond repair.

When the sun went down and the air grew cold I built a fire with logs from old olive trees or their gnarled roots. Both for heat and fragrance these make a splendid fuel, better than the eucalyptus gum-tree and as good as the hard black turf of western Ireland. Puri would be screeching away in the kitchen as she fried the eggs for supper. From the ventilation holes round the tiled fireplace peeped the merry little eyes of mice, witty Spanish mice who loved to gnaw a typewriter ribbon through and festoon it about the room, or munch a manuscript. The moon rose over the sea. The whump whump whump! of the motor trawler began and, irritating and reassuring at once, would continue until the dawn. The lamps of fishing boats danced up and down on the waves and the ragged line of the Sierras north of Malaga were black against the darkened sky. Owls hooted in the garden.

On Sundays the sounds of rustic pleasure would come faintly down from Arroyo itself. Sunday evenings anywhere have a flavour all their own, a feel of vague delicious melancholy as if we then were particularly aware of and resigned to the passing of time. The instant the meal was done I would settle to a book beside the fire. What more could the heart of man wish for? But all too often, just when I had found my page and Puri was setting out to join her friends in the village, the lights would go out. Puri always shrieked with joy: she never cared what happened, as long as something did. The electric current failed three or four times a week as a matter of habit, with extra bouts if a gale were blowing. There were supposed to be candles and matches at strategic points throughout the house, but there never were. Puri saw to that: prudence, forethought, she could not abide and liked everything à l'impromptu with the maximum of pleasure and shouting and inconvenience. She would scream delightedly that ¡madre de Dios! the mice had eaten all the candles. Next she would throw up the window and in her horrendous voice implore our neighbour to concede us some of hers. Deadlock ensued at that, for neither our neighbour nor Puri would walk through the darkness alone. Then Puri screamed for Antonio who did not mind darkness as long as he need not pass the cemetery in it; but that old badger was ruminating in his earth and made no reply. Silence fell and continued until an appalling stench from the kitchen would reveal that Puri was improvising a lantern with rags steeped in the precious olive oil. Up in the village the sounds of merry-making had given way to howls of rage, as well they might, for the current would never come on before midnight and the few hours on Sunday night were all the people had for enjoying themselves.

Many an evening I spent by the fragrant burning logs, contemplating the ruins of the evening and the malicious little faces of the mice. For anyone anxious to acquire the merit of non-attachment Spain is the place to go. The mind grows supple from the sheer unpredictability of things and the heart finds peace in consent: habit falls away and man wandereth freely under the stars. The fire would slowly burn away and when it was dead I groped my way upstairs and lay awake till the light came on and blazed all over the house and the village and the province of Malaga at two, three or four in the morning, as suited its fancy.

❧ 2 ❧

AFTER A SHORT TIME IN ARROYO, IN ALMOST NO TIME AT all, the wish to go anywhere else quietly died. This is another difference between the resident and the peripatetic. Freed from the concierge's goad and the competition of fellow travellers, and with an apparently endless row of to-morrows stretching away ahead, one contentedly takes one's ease like any old turnip in a field.

There is a singular relish to life that is always the same. Every morning before it was light mules went down the track by the *finca* to the shore for loads of sand. They were better than an alarm clock and woke me at just the moment to see the sunrise. Presently the haunting smell of burnt oil spread through the house, together with that vigorous fanning which is a characteristic sound of Spanish houses and must, I believe, have inspired the 'Ritual Fire Dance' in de Falla's *El Amor Brujo*. Puri was lighting the brazier by the immemorial and highly inconvenient methods of her people. She put an oily rag under the charcoal and lit it, fanning excitedly as it smouldered until the charcoal reddened and glowed and after much more fanning at last took fire. In another half an hour or so it would be hot enough to bring a small pannikin of water to the boil. One day I walked into the kitchen as she was about to embark on this procedure and said I would show her something. I arranged a few paper spills and dry twigs in the brazier and piled charcoal over them, as one would set a fire at home. The twigs instantly caught light, the flames leaped up, the charcoal crackled and spat, there was no smell and the coffee

18

was ready in no time. Puri said nothing, but she was not herself for the whole of that day. Her sense of fitness as well as her conservatism had been outraged and next morning the familiar stench crept up the stairs at the usual hour accompanied by the de Fallaesque humming of the fan.

Nothing would have induced her to change her habits, even if I had not learned my lesson and left her in peace. She washed everything however oily in cold water and without soap, merely scouring the pots, pans, china, silver and all with a bunch of coarse fibre-like dried grass. Some of it came away with each use so that eventually, inevitably, the drainpipe was blocked and we sent for the *fontanero*, as the plumber was called. He may in fact have been too busy making fountains, for he never came until appealed to a third or fourth time and it was clear that he thought a stopped kitchen-sink beneath his attention and ours. In cold water too, on hands and knees, Puri slowly washed all the stone floors in the house once a day, including those in rooms never used and therefore as clean as a whistle; and in cold water did the entire laundry, sheets and all, rubbing and slapping things against a ridged board until the dirt was worn away rather than expelled. All preparations of food were carried out in the most time-consuming and uncomfortable way that the human mind could imagine. The little gadgets I brought from Gibraltar, the slicers, peelers, graters, mincers, were left to rust while Puri chopped and scraped with one of the bluntest knives in creation: she would employ no labour-saving device more intricate or up-to-the-minute than a mortar and pestle.

In the beginning her mindless techniques annoyed me, then they amused; with time I came round to them and, at last, I believe I understood them. They left her brain free to dwell on the splendours of her *novio* and the felicity awaiting her when she should become his wife. Every time she had to wrench it from this contemplation and waste it, however briefly, on something non-essential like work it was an agony

19

to her. The only interruption she could endure was some human encounter, such as a fish or vegetable man or a gipsy coming to the door, when the wag of her tongue would be as brisk and to the point as her bodily movements were languid and dissociated. And this long dream may have been the whole brightness of her life, if she went the usual way of peasant women in her country.

While it is natural for girls anywhere to think about young men, in its removal of all objects but one from her mind Puri's concentration was peculiarly Spanish. For most Spaniards one idea at a time is plenty, a fact which clearly comes home when we raise a matter with them while they are engaged on something else. It is a quality that may richly bear fruit but may also act as a kind of spiritual barricade, preventing equally the expulsion of a fixed idea and the entry of one that is new. It may produce a Teresa of Avila or a St John of the Cross; and it can, and rather more often does, result in dear Puri.

And in this way the time slipped gently by. Now and then I walked over the hills to visit my friends in Churriana. It was a distance of seven or eight miles and there were always things on the road to catch the eye or incidents to engage the mind. Dogs rushed out from the little peasant dwellings near and and far with the curious weaving motion of the body they have when they mean business, too intent on their plans to bark. It was a point for eager speculation whether the owners would call them off before they reached their goal or not. Often on a lonely trip I would encounter a family of gipsies moving camp. The man would always be riding a little ahead of the others, frequently on a good horse, and he wore a wide black hat at a rakish angle and, to keep his chest and shoulders warm, a coloured blanket with holes for head and arms, as Mexicans wear the *poncho*: in fact, there was a touch of Mexico about the entire scene as the rider trotted haughtily on through the heavy white dust and past the tall agave plants with their fleshy thorny glaucous leaves. The women and children followed him, either stumbling along on foot or on a mule, dragging with them their pots and pans and little household treasures. None of the gipsies ever molested strangers out here in the wilds, in contrast to their behaviour in towns where the women at least would whine and cajole and curse until they got their way. Now they merely threw a glance or two from bright shallow eyes and muttered a perfunctory greeting. On one occasion as I rounded a corner I came face to face with a black bull of tremendous size and with wide sweeping horns like the bulls in the arena. For a moment or two we considered each other and then he lowered his great curly head and began to dig the ground with his hoofs, for all the world as if he had seen it done on television. Now was the time to cry ¡Je, toro! or do a veronica or perform any one of those simple effective rites but all seemed different here. Instinct told me this bull would never, never catch the spirit of *la lidia*. I tried the old familiar swank-piece of turning away from the bull and strutting off, but the strut became a lope in spite of me and there was none of the frenzied applause. After a while I plucked up my courage and looked round. The bull had lost what interest he ever had and was quietly cropping grass.

At one point it was necessary to fork away to the left if one were not to drift along Calvario and end up in Torremolinos, and here the grim bulk of the reformatory, like a miniature Escorial, acted as signpost. The reformatory was run by Franciscans, rosy-faced and white-bearded old men apparently on the best of terms with life. I once saw a particularly plump and jovial one administer a stinging box on the ear to a boy without the slightest change in his merry countenance, and another day I ran into a little posse of them returning flushed and giggling from a spree. Well to the left of their fortress was now the way to go, skirting a spinney of fir with a ball of silvery fluff on nearly every bough like ornaments on a sinister kind of Christmas tree, along the track and past the waterman's house with its flowery pool where shoals of

chubby carp shot to and fro and its air of drowsing charm and
decay like an old buried house in a novel by Turgenev, on
over heavy clays of red, cinnamon or yellow and through a
scrubby rocky terrain planted with olive to the *carretera* which
ran from the coastal road up a long fertile valley of almond
and peach past Alhaurin el Grande to Coin.

Often the winter rains did terrible things to this hill. They
cut deep gashes in its side or hurled boulders down it in a
flood, washing bare the roots of the olives. Then every man
turned out to help, for olives come so slowly into fruiting that
to lose a single tree is a serious matter: the old Greek practice
of felling the entire groves of defeated enemies would hardly
occur to a Spaniard, I think. In those wild winter storms
houses and bridges collapsed as well, cliffs toppled over and
caves fell in, oranges and lemons were blown from their trees
by the ton and the land as a whole wore a look of huge despoil-
ing and ravaging. On one occasion the main street of Churriana
became a torrent three feet deep and people have been drowned
in this village where during the summer, as in most of Andalusia, water has to be husbanded with the greatest care.

At times it was hard to imagine why the term "Costa del
Sol" had ever been bestowed on this weeping desert. Then
almost from one moment to the next the sun came out and the
land was wreathed in smiles again. Walking the rough track
on the hill was like walking in Eden itself, with the flower-blue
sea on the right and the tawny crumpled hills ahead. Now and
again a glimpse of snowy peaks appeared, the rosy dazzling
Sierras of Granada far away to the north, gladdening the soul
like a glimpse of the Delectable Mountains. It quickly grew
warm and shepherds lay under the trees asleep or talking and
smoking, their drowsy dogs at their side with one eye open for
a confused or flighty sheep. Women washed clothes in the
little brooks that ran down the hillside and impaled them on
thorn bushes to dry while their children frolicked round them
and birds sang.

Then there was the *carretera* and the road down to the village, past the tall tremulous eucalyptus to the long line of white houses. My friends the Brenans lived in one of them, or part of one, for the rest had been let for a song by a well-intentioned caretaker in the troubled times following the Civil War. As a rule the tenants were not to be seen and a tomb-like silence reigned over the house.

Even the front door was in their possession. Visitors went through a side door past the gardener's lodge and there sat his wife, Rosario, alert as a spider and not wholly dissimilar in shape, on a chair outside her door with hens and cocks clucking and pecking round her feet. Rosario loved barnyard fowl and used to believe that she could not exist without them. Subsequently two lots died rapidly off from the pest and she decided that, after all, only pigs were necessary to life. Mingling fraternally with the hens were a flock of white doves, whose dovecot was in a great tree nearby. Their cooing and the whisper of a fountain in the courtyard were the first sounds to catch the ear. The fountain played without stopping, for the house had formerly belonged to a nobleman and the unrestricted use of water was an ancient right that went with it.

Rosario came from the mountain village in the Alpujarra which Gerald Brenan magnificently describes in *South from Granada*. She was a mixture of shrewdness, calculation, devotion and benevolence and had a delightfully astringent tongue. She used to tell me, before I asked, if the Señores were out or in, or in but with strangers. When that was the case I retired to the look-out on the far wall and enjoyed the beauties of the garden or the view outwards, over the blue-green artichokes in the field below and the farmhouse with the sentinel trees that I had dreamed of buying until the Jesuits nipped in before me, and beyond the *pueblo* that spilled out in low white blocks across the *vega* to the mountains beyond. Callers came thick and fast all the year round, eager to meet the eminent author and in the happy assumption that he would be no less eager to meet them.

Sometimes I was already in when they appeared and retreat was cut off. Strange indeed were the forms of life that strewed Mr Brenan's beautiful house while he plied them with delicious China tea and daunting local pastries. One of them was a woman psychiatrist who was busy on research into anxiety conditions of the Andalusian peasant, Andalusia being about the very last place in Europe where conditions of anxiety in her sense could hope to thrive. Within a minute or two of her arrival she took Gerald Brenan to task for certain of his views on Spain, a country in which he had lived for thirty years.

It has been held that pleasure is the absence of pain and after an encounter with one of these exotics the usual contentment I felt at being in Spain would turn to active delight. I would contemplate then rather than take for granted her manifold excellence, both in the wonderful things that she was and the dreadful things she was not. A happy frame of mind could also be induced by picking up a newspaper from home, running an eye over the breezy or sententious text and putting it down again.

Sometimes there was no one at home but the Brenans and the three cats. Cats stood between Mrs Brenan and me: she loved them deeply and entered with whole heart into their nasty little lives, their hysterical attachments, their phantom pregnancies, their insane grievances and eternal grudges. The mice in my *casita* were Spanish to the core but these cats were just cats, universal cats, esperanto cats. How could she? But then how could I bear a bull-fight? There is often something like this in friendship. Mrs Brenan was also Gamel Woolsey who wrote exquisite poetry and translated admirably from the Spanish. She was a capital companion, being game for anything and a mistress of lapidary speech, a gift I have noted before in the wives of literary men and due no doubt to their restricted opportunities of getting a word in at all.

Life in that household used to flow along like some broad

deep river. No one worried about anything, least of all the passing of time. Rosario went to market and cooked, and her two daughters cleaned and waited at table. The elder of these, Maria, with her strong brows and calm oval face, was like the Madonna in one of the primitive glass paintings that hung in the study. On the street side of the house was all the Spanish hurly-burly, the Vespas scorching up the road with the silencers removed, the slow rumbling carts, the snatches of *flamenco*, the screamed conversation of women, the tormented utterance of donkeys, the dainty fluttering of goats' feet, the hoarse cry of a pedlar or the knife-grinder's fluting pipes. At the back was perfect peace, in the old walled garden with the orange and lemon and fig trees, the datura with its great snowy flower-trumpets, the crimson-tasselled banana, the shrubs, the roses and the rich blue morning glory. One of the highlights was a mighty pecan-tree, afterwards uprooted on a Christmas Eve by a tornado which also accounted for the tall pepper and the massive, creepered and highly romantic double arch over a well in the very middle of the garden. Antonio was usually at work there, digging or irrigating, a small taciturn man who rarely smiled. The professional melancholy of the gardener was heightened in him by severe headaches and the preponderance in his family of the feminine. He worked on a share-crop basis and provided fruit and cut flowers the year round, with peak periods of activity at Easter and in the autumn, when he grew rows of wan lugubrious chrysanthemums for All Souls' Day.

It was a patrician house where taste mingled with simplicity and worthwhile things were achieved without vulgar haste. Gerald Brenan believed that to write one letter was ample occupation for a morning, and a novel engaged him for thirty years. Convention barred his wife from the kitchen except on one day of the year when she broke in and willy-nilly made marmalade of bitter orange: otherwise she typed the masterpieces that fell from her husband's pen, in a reckless yet vivid and engaging style that did for English orthography and punctuation what some Caribbean writers have done for the language itself, and, whatever the merits of the case, was infinitely charming to the stream of callers.

The time I am speaking of was only five or six years ago and yet everything has changed enormously for the better, as in many parts of Spain. Then there were few buses to Malaga in the day, and those nearly empty: now they run frequently and are so tightly crammed with people that it is hard to breathe. Now the village girls look much like girls anywhere: in those days a ragged cotton dress and no stockings or shoes was the common wear, although a blossoming would occur on Sunday or at a fiesta. Then too Gamel Brenan and I would no sooner be out of the lodge gate than some woman or other would sidle up and ask for money. They were not actual beggars but hard luck cases, and as such too high to attend the communal alms-giving that took place in patriarchal fashion at the house every Saturday. Mrs Brenan shared one characteristic with the manatee, or sea-cow: nature had left her without any defence against anything whatsoever. Like that plaintive sighing mammal she had no claw, no horn, no poison-fang, no tentacle, no suffocating coil or shattering hug: there was nothing for it in times of peril but to resign herself or flee. She could neither refuse the women money nor prevent them from kissing her when she gave it. We used to wait peeping through the crack of the gate until the road seemed to be clear, although one female grenadier there was who paced up and down until we came out.

There were many delightful walks round about, either arduous or gentle. We could go up to the cross-roads, on the grass verges of which the gipsies would camp and women loved to spread their washing to dry, where it could depend on attracting clouds of dust from the traffic and the attentions of every stray dog. There we turned right in the direction of Coin, a small town up the valley where the dancer Antonio in

26

fact was born, although Malaga claims him, and where we had always meant to go together and to this day never did. It was prudent to leave the highway as soon as might be, for giant lorries roared along it at a terrific speed and with horrible noise, those oncoming every now and again swerving out from their side for a look at us. Tracks led away from it each side, up towards the mountains, among the olives, down the slope by banks of asphodel and along gullies with the tenacious oleander sucking at every moist patch. Some way down was a property belonging to a nobleman which had imposing gates that seemed to warn the plebs to keep out while beside them the ruined wall with its stones tumbled about the earth invited them in. Further on was capital ground for botanical prizes, where the blue ground-iris and rock rose bloomed earlier than elsewhere in the valley. A sweep round brought us into the lower end of the village, past the cemetery with its marbled tombs for some and holes in the wall for others, to the first low white cottages where old women sat round the door with dogs and bare-bottomed children crawling at their feet, over the brackish stream which was Churriana's principal laundry, on to the attractive house with the *chirimoyo* trees that the two old ladies would regularly offer for sale and as regularly withdraw again and into the curving main street of Churriana.

The village was anything but a hub of commerce. There were one or two little shops, a café, a wineshop, the pharmacy and the Post Office, under the care of a dour middle-aged woman who eyed her customers severely until they had tipped her. The tip did not have to be large and it produced an effect of radiance as magically as if she had been an automatic machine with coin-box attached. It was hard to say if she were professionally skilled or dedicated. Frequently it happened that people got to the village a day or so ahead of the telegram announcing their arrival, but that is nothing. Spaniards feel differently in these matters. A packet of coffee sent from London once took two and a half months on the road to Malaga

27

and when I went to collect it they waved me to the reception office for parcels sent at "gran velocidad". Opposite that I noticed an office for those of "pequeña velocidad", and went my way marvelling.

The *farmacia* throve, as is usual even in small places, for few Spanish doctors think their work is done until they have prescribed four or five remedies to the case. Once I was laid up in Churriana with a tired heart and the doctor ordered pills before food and pills after it, pills first thing in the morning and suppositories last thing at night: and, needless to say, injections. These were administered by the *practicante* or male nurse. There would be the roar of a motor-bicycle, followed by the louder roar of a genial voice teasing Rosario and the tread of heavy feet in the yard and up the stairs, whereupon a burly red-faced man in beret and muffler would burst into the room, laughingly stab my flinching buttock and rush away. It was like a daily visit from a whirlwind. Don José the doctor was quiet, with a boy's face and melancholy blue eyes, and he was very small, so small that it led to an awkwardness at the first visit. I called out for him to come in when he knocked on the bedroom door, but nothing seemed to happen and thinking he had not heard I called again just as, with tremendous dignity, he marched into view round the foot of the big Spanish bed.

Don José was a clever doctor, like a predecessor of his called Don José as well. A wealthy foreign patient of the earlier Don José once asked if he might call a specialist from London and was told to go ahead. The great man arrived and, after careful examination, said that he agreed with his Spanish colleague. Asked what ought to be done, he said that his colleague's treatment should be continued. A large amount of money changed hands and the consultant flew away. Don José went on with his work and sent in a bill for a few pesetas now and then, if he thought of it. When the cure was complete his thankful client presented him with a pianola and on this, enchanted, he would play for hours at a time.

After the *farmacia* came the last lap of the old white road with its dust and dung and the open drain into which refuse of all kinds found a way. Over it hung an aroma associated peculiarly in my mind with Spain, even though it is to be enjoyed in many other lands as well. An Englishman who lived there once said he could never, while travelling abroad, pass an open sewer without a pang of nostalgia; and I knew exactly what he meant. "Just when we're safest, there's a sunset touch. . . ." And as I write these words a vision comes, an enchanting still-life of broken glass and pomegranate rinds with a dead rat floating in iridescent water, and beckons to me sweetly.

In the garden there was wine to drink and olives cured in garlic. Rosario believed in garlic and her guests left the house fairly reeking of it. She was a good cook in an earthy way, and indeed Spanish food is best when earthy: coarse bread and strong cheese, *fabadas* and *caldos*, *chorizos* and *tortillas*. One of Rosario's specialities was potato stewed to a mush in oil and flavoured with dill, which she may have brought from her far mountain village, as I never met it anywhere else; and another was the homely *puchero*. In *South from Granada* Mr Brenan describes this, the national dish of Castile and usually called *cocido* there, in the following terms: "This is a boiled affair, not unlike the French *pot-au-feu*, of which the essential ingredients are pork, chunks of *tocino* or bacon fat, potatoes, turnips and chick peas. The chick pea, from which Cicero took his name, is a yellow bullet which explodes in the inside into several cubic feet of gas, while if the cook knows her job properly she will see that the meat is boiled till it has no taste left and that the fat, a yellowish white in colour, is rancid. A Spaniard feels when he eats this dish that he has vindicated his toughness of fibre. He has not yet degenerated from the breed of men who conquered a continent with a handful of adventurers, wore hair shirts day and night till they stuck to their flesh, and braved the mosquitoes of the Pilcomayo and the Amazon." I quote this for the delightful *bravura,* but there are one or two small inaccuracies in it. *Tocino* and chick peas are the only essential ingredients and any white meat or root vegetable can be used; and the prolonged boiling, with a piece of bone, not with the meat, is required to soften the chick peas, which otherwise in spite of having soaked overnight would not explode into anything at all but lie on the stomach like yellow pebbles. Furthermore, *puchero* is delicious, and my heart would rejoice to see Carmen tripping over the yard with a plump tureen containing the broth, to be drunk beforehand separately. The amusing thing was that in spite of Don Geraldo's bitter remarks in the book, Rosario served up *puchero* more often than anything else, more even than the fresh sardines split open, tied together in bunches by the tails and fried in oil, another delectable stand-by of hers. The eminent *padrón* did not comment on this or fail to eat his share: perhaps the issue had already come to a head between them and Rosario had won, or it may have been that, as with many of us towards *cosas de España*, his theory bore no relation to his practice.

Merely to describe a Churriana meal fills me with an emotion like that of Proust as he tasted the famous little madeleine soaked in tea. Not for the world would I have had one detail of it altered, even the fact that nothing was ever hot. Hot food and drink is in any case a northern fad, despised by the fortunate dwellers round the Mediterranean, and as everything had to be cooked in Rosario's kitchen her lukewarm dishes had every opportunity to cool off further as they were carried through the garden.

The main dish was followed by a salad, made of lettuce limp and transparent with oil and of tomato in a pond of lemony water and rife with garlic. This heap of dank vegetation was not special to the house but conformed to the ideal of *ensalada* that prevails throughout Spain. If anyone had recently been to Malaga there then came cheese, harsh *manchego* or suave curd, with some of the sweetest butter to be found anywhere; and a plate of oranges, the little insipid ones of Malaga known as *dulces* and the fine big sharp ones of Valencia called *ácidas*. The Malagueños carry local patriotism to the extreme of preferring their own to the others.

The meal ended with coffee and *un petit verre*. Carmen went down the road to fetch the post and collect gossip about those trifling daily events that are so delightful and absorbing. The doves fell asleep and the clumsily moving bats whirled and swooped against the faded sky. The ritual of feeding the cats and the tiny dramas connected with it were slowly accomplished. Opinions were canvassed as to whether Gris-gris could really be pregnant again so soon. The moon rose, branches stirred fitfully in the breeze, the fountain chattered away in a low voice, an owl hooted in the great elm: here if anywhere in the world something like absolute peace was to be found.

❧ 3 ❧

ONCE A MONTH, OR AS OFTEN AS I WOULD BEAR IT, THE
rhythm of our life was interrupted while Puri, screaming like a
jay, whitewashed the house inside and out, chimneys and all. It
never looked otherwise than snowy, but the news that someone
up the hill intended to whitewash hers would goad her into a
fever of envy and emulation. At these times she could just
manage to put the breakfast coffee on the table, but only let the
sound of dragging steps and discontented muttering notify
her that Antonio was in the yard to mix the pails of *yeso* and
bring the ladders up and all else flew out of her head. Then I
would drink my coffee, hide books, papers and clothes beyond
the range of her dripping brush and set out on one of the
expeditions that otherwise were continually postponed from
day to day.

The road from Algeciras to Malaga passed fifty yards from
the house but there were only two coaches a day that would
stop. To get to Malaga it was necessary either to walk three
miles to Torremolinos and catch the bus; or go a mile up to
Arroyo de la Miel station, leaping ravines, warding off dogs
and threading a way through the laundry spread over the
ground to dry and bleach in the sun, and catch the little train
that beetled along from Fuengirola to Arroyo, on to Torremolinos and along the coast, past sugar-cane and eucalyptus
and small dark soldiers in cotton uniforms who appeared to
be in hard, resolute training for the Peninsular War. It all took
an immense amount of time, and consequently I came to know
the various local taximen quite well. Their rank was in the

plaza at Torremolinos, where they sat and smoked and chatted, with one sardonic eye on the foreign population. Most of them seemed to be called Antonio and they were as kind and patient as men could be. Without extra charge they waited outside café or shop in the contented languor that comes so naturally to Andalusians and on reaching their passenger's house would carry each parcel in, to the last stick of bread. Whatever the old Spain hands may say, Spanish men are extremely gallant and helpful to women—provided, of course, that no one is looking on. One day I heard with amazement that one of these amiable fellows had knocked a foreigner down in a Torremolinos bar and kicked out his eye as he lay on the floor. When it happened I was about to leave for Madrid and so never found out which of them had done it, but I wonder to this day what the provocation can have been. In a great many Spaniards there is a sleeping volcano which it is a mistake to ignore.

It is hard to write or speak or even think of Torremolinos without a feeling of melancholy. More than anything it resembles a town in an occupied country where the conquerors go their way and take the best of everything while the vanquished lead a worried little life under cover and out of sight. It used to be a small fishing village like many others on the Costa del Sol, except that a few discerning people were in the habit of spending their summers there. Low white cottages sprawled down a slope to the sea: brown fishing nets of a salty fragrance dried in the sun over boats upturned at the water's edge or hung from oars planted in the sand: the mountains lowered in the background and in front was the sea with now and then on a clear day a glimpse, or just an intimation, of Africa. To look at it now and at the country round about is like looking at the face of a friend suddenly struck with not one but every affliction of the skin: warts, wens, carbuncles, leprosy, lupus, pox; and, as with a friend, we mourn and puzzle as to why it should thus be singled out. Nightmarish villas rise from the ground with the alacrity of toadstools so that every month the aspect is different and worse, and hotels, giftshops, bars, night-clubs, hairdressers, are gleefully making hay. Signboards and posters are drawn up in foreign tongues, again as under a military occupation. Outside the fish and vegetable market is a notice calling on the people to dispose of their garbage and keep their streets clean "in a manner appropriate to their tourist category".

People of many nations swarm here, as well as of many kinds and different ages and social extremes. A man will be pointed out with awe as having made even Tangier too hot to hold him. A faded little woman from outer London, who has saved hard for the fare out and the unsuitable pantaloons she wears, will look wistfully at the gay crowd of bogus painters and writers, longing to be noticed and welcomed and asked round for a little marijuana. There are retired empire-builders, pimps still very much on the active list, landscape gardeners, pugilists. And yet, in an odd way, the people here tend to look alike. Introduced, one feels that one has met them before but remembers nothing apart from that: one gives strangers and detrimentals an effusive greeting and looks straight through those nice friends of friends who so kindly had asked one in to cocktails the evening before.

On one occasion I saw the gulf between the owners and the interlopers bridged, if only for a moment. Everything was just as usual. The street lamps all were fiercely burning although it was the middle of a sunny morning. Tourists drank outside the Central or the Jerez, donkeys from the grey stone fountain in the *plaza*. A Spanish youth on a Vespa talked to his companions, revving his engine meanwhile for the sake of the lovely music. Two lean *Guardias Civiles* patrolled the main street, one on either side, brown faces under black shiny hats, rifles slung, grave, silent, looking at nobody. The fat policeman in grey was rubbing the middle button of his tunic against his favourite bar. A tiny car drew up and eight Spaniards poured out of it. The Mañana night-club announced Calypso for that

34

evening, instead of the *flamenco* of which foreigners, unlike Andalusians, occasionally tire. In Manolo's a peer and peeress were eagerly watching life go by, the lady's head in a basket for fear of sun and wind. The ex-Gestapo man continually bowed and clicked his heels and bared his teeth and the retired English general was happily engaged with beer and prawns and a book on spiritualism.

An elderly couple dropped into chairs beside me and the woman clapped for the waiter in an obsolete way. "Ooner cognac et puis ooner café y doh tassers," she said fluently in her Kensington voice. "Y agua chaud pour le Signore porque café too forte per lui . . ." The husband frowned and said, "Doesn't the fellow talk English?" She answered with quiet dignity, "Thank you, Harold, I am doing very well with my Spanish."

An American with a long beard vaulted on to the rump of a mule already overladen and, deaf to the owner's cries, rode it away up Calvario. The poet with the bush of hair was fast asleep, dead drunk, and the catamite from Tetuan in the silver sharkskin drawers was pouting at his liege. Great Spanish lorries thundered through the town without lowering their speed as if it were one of the cities of the plain. A slight commotion broke out, there were agitated murmurs here and there among the people, and plunging and rearing among the mules, as a glossy motor-coach drew up crammed with Swedes who had concealed themselves behind pink beaming masks and were waving rattles. Pleased with their little effect, they lowered the masks as one man from their anxious pallid faces and smiled in deprecation through the windows.

Now there came tripping along a chubby person with a round face and eyes like two plums, wearing her tinted hair in a childish stream down her back. She was dressed in a pair of man's checked trousers so tight as to flatten her promontories and a man's yellow cardigan that, for some occult purpose, was back to front. On her head was a wide *sombrero*

35

with a yellow foulard swathed about it and falling in tails behind, and from her neck a chain as heavy as a Lord Mayor's fell to her knees. She walked on immensely high-heeled shoes, resulting in a mincing kind of gait that did not harmonize with her build.

To catch the eye in Torremolinos is no small achievement, but somehow this woman brought it off. The arresting thing perhaps was not so much the garb as the confidence of the wearer. A famous beauty, dressed by Balenciaga, could not have looked more self-enchanted than this figure of fun as it tottered purposefully towards a bar. The spectacle was a privilege as well as a treat and more, as I have said, it was an occasion. It drew all present, Spaniard and foreigner alike, together in spontaneous mirth and not a straight face was to be seen in that busy square. For a moment the two worlds had joined hands.

But I never saw this unity before or since: by common consent a kind of *apartheid* is maintained. The stream of Spanish life flows on under the nonsense like a violin sonata on the radio that is all but smothered by a neighbouring programme of jazz. Suddenly round the corner from the little *plaza* with its church and into San Miguel will come a religious procession or a funeral, picking its way through the foreign cars and looking curiously out of place. The foreigners stare idly at it without lowering their voices or putting away their cigarettes. If it is a funeral they may wonder idly which of the toothless old men or the bowed women they have seen about it may be. Or perhaps someone will say, "Didn't you hear, it is that nice girl in the hardware, it seems she complained of headache at noon and was dead at six": and they vaguely remember a dark rosy girl of endless humour and tact whose mission was to sell them glasses and corkscrews and who had no business to go off and suit herself in that flighty manner. The mules with their bulging panniers and scarred bleeding backs trudge through the town with owners who proceed on their way calm and unhurrying

36

as if no traffic were there and who hail each other as if only they existed. Little girls go in bridal attire to their First Communion, snowily gloved and veiled, fairy-like creatures tripping through the wasteland of shorts and bikinis and chubby old ladies in slacks: or a hired lorry will convey the male youth, packed like a barrel of dried figs and fervently shouting, to a football match at Marbella or Fuengirola. As the sun goes down and the cool of the evening follows and the strangers are gathered up in the endless parties that are always the same, out come the families to sit round the doors in the old Spanish way and muse on the day's events at their ease.

But these Spaniards that appear so fleetingly and intermittently remain gloriously themselves. As Cánovas, the nineteenth-century statesman, remarked long ago, everything collapses in Spain except the race, and indeed this race is indestructible and incorruptible. This is not to say they spurn the rewards of tourism: far from it, they are up to every little dodge that ingenuity can devise. But, priceless gift, they milk the foreigner without losing a jot of their inner wholeness and contemplate his better fortune without any intention of copying his ways. What other people ravaged and savaged by tourist hordes can claim as much? Blessed are the pure in heart. The glory of Torremolinos is to have inwardly survived its ruin.

Much as I disliked the place, it was necessary to go there if I wanted a car at a reasonable rate. The alternative was to telephone the cab-rank from a smart hotel by the sea just near the *casita*; and after the driver had pulled up outside its impressive shining door and sent in a supercilious page to announce his arrival he considered any kind of financial argument unworthy of us both. One of the Antonios had a contemporary Buick with a powerful engine, which was the very thing for travelling the steep and twisting mountain roads of the region. On the eve of one of Puri's whitewashing frenzies I took the trouble to walk all the way in and fix with him, man to man, for a trip to Mijas. The price was agreed and an hour appointed, but

Antonio secretly feared for his paint and next day a complete stranger drew up at my porch with about the seediest old jalopy in the province. With the radiator a-bubble and a-fume it crawled up the steep winding roads at a snail's pace, growing ever slower and slower until I was sure it would stop and the brakes would fail and all would roll comfortably over the edge of the cliff together. Ever and anon the driver would take both hands off the wheel to light a cigarette, in the provoking manner of his kind. One of my recurring nightmares is of driving in Spanish mountains in an old Spanish taxi and with just such a Spanish fatalist at the wheel: it comes round nearly as often as the one where I step out of an aeroplane on to a cloud. And in real life I have done it scores of times without the terror ever growing less. It is of no use to comfort oneself by saying that it is all right and nothing will happen, because it is not all right and things do happen all the time.

That day was a lucky one, however, and it was beautiful as well, a day of early March when the land was covering itself with flowers. Everywhere were the crinkled papery roses of the cistus, white or purple, the blue of ground-iris against pink peach blossom and clumps of asphodel with bloom like bubbles of soap. Mijas was a typical Andalusian hill town with narrow cobbled streets running through it and houses washed so white that in the shadow they looked blue: houses bare and un-cluttered like Spanish landscape and Spanish life itself. At every corner or opening in a wall there were magnificent views over the plain far below or over the sea, dark, oil-smooth and streaked as if slashed by satiny ribbons.

A little band of grave-eyed children followed everywhere about, Victoria, Juan-Jesús, Pepe, Alonzo and their leader Salvador, who beat the others about the head when they asked for pesetas. He was admirably firm on the point but when at last they said good-bye he extended his own hard little paw in a way that was not to be overlooked. The mood of the town that afternoon was one of innocent gaiety. People smiled out from doorways and old women sat on chairs in the street, plaiting baskets and tossing jokes to each other in reedy voices. There was a memorial garden to the dead of the Civil War on the edge of the town with a chapel hewn out of the rock and an iron grille across the entrance, and inside an unkempt altar with vases of dead flowers and candle grease spilled on the cloth. A party of young girls in Sunday frocks came there chattering like starlings, flung themselves on their knees at the grille and recited a few Aves in the metallic drone they keep for this purpose before tearing off again, screaming and laughing. The men, however, maintained their usual impassive front demeanour and, dressed in corduroy suits and broad black hats, looked out from the dusty taverns hour after hour, silent, neither drinking nor playing cards, as if merely waiting for the end of the world.

I wonder how it would be to belong to one of these rural communities that make so agreeable an impression on the outsider. There is a novel by José Camilo Cela, *Molino de Viento*, which gives a horrifying picture of a *pueblo* from the inside, a welter of cruelty, envy, spite and despair, and of a deadening sameness that the author expresses by taking the characters up and throwing them down, taking them up, throwing them down, one after the other on and on until one feels in his prose the endless implacable sweep of the windmill's arms. It is an amazing and dreadful book, but one of great power and vitality; but when I consulted Spanish friends as to its truth, needless to say they had never heard of it.

For an afternoon, however, Mijas was perfection. The sky was unclouded and the sun almost hot and the lizards were out in scores. After visiting the agate mine and the church and drinking in the stupendous views again I went for a glass of beer in one of the cafés before going home. The old gentlemen established there disdainfully looked away, while the *padrón* could not take his eyes off me and stood pouring beer on the table instead of into the glass.

39

The demon driver was curled up in the taxi, asleep, exhausted by the rigours and perils of the ascent. As we set off down the mountainside the engine moaned and died in all too familiar a fashion. The driver said proudly that it was nearly fifteen years old, a statement I did not for a moment query, and releasing the brake he allowed the car to hurtle down a few yards, only to brake again with such violence that I hit my head against the roof. He repeated this a few times more until the engine consented to fire and we went on our way, swaying and bumping, my mind disturbed by a haunting smell of burnt rubber. The driver employed the customary technique at steep blind corners, which is to sound the horn and step on the gas, and, avid for conversation, could hardly bring himself to look at the road at all.

Thanks to Puri I was hounded forth not only to Mijas but to Ronda and Coin as well, all places of beauty and interest that left to myself I should never have dreamed of visiting. Now and again, too, I went as far as Gibraltar, in the early coach that drove with frequent stops along the writhing coastal road of which every turn and twist and tree and rock was familiar until the huge grey mass came into view, dramatic as always. I never could see the white *pueblo* of San Roque sprawling over the green hill opposite it without mentally dipping the colours. Once, when the squabble over Gibraltar had blown up again, its mayor had wired to General Franco the gallant message: "Say the word, Caudillo, and San Roque will march." The mind recoils from the thought of what might happen were the *Generalísimo* to say the word, for if Don Quixote is as alive to-day as ever so too is Sancho Panza and it is by no means unusual to find the pair of them uneasily yoked together in a single heart.

It was often wet in Gibraltar and the first quick impression might be an English one, what with the driving rain and the waving umbrellas, not to speak of the policemen's helmets and Boots the Chemist and Lipton the Grocer and Gieves the

Outfitter; and men being unostentatiously polite to women and demonstratively kind to dogs. But then the sun always seemed to break through and the square was gay with flowers, lottery tickets were everywhere on sale, sloe-eyed girls with Spanish accents sold the marmalade and the Gentlemen's Relish, while Hindus, Jews and Muslims cajoled and wheedled from the doorways of their bazaars. It has always been an uncomfortable place, spiritually and physically, being far too narrow for different kinds of people thinking different kinds of thoughts and walked about at different speeds. The apes on the rock are about as integrated and adjusted as anyone there can hope to be.

Yet it always provided food for thought, for things there were well done and, no doubt of it, there is a great beauty in things done well. The guard at the Governor's house was smart and soldierly, the great aeroplanes landed perfectly and perfectly took off, the ships lying at anchor were models of order and cleanliness; and among the tawdry junk in the bazaars were all kinds of alien treasures, knives that cut, fabrics that lasted, soap that washed, gadgets that worked. There is little in Spain that works or lasts and it is not generally the custom to do things well: indeed the only exceptions that directly spring to mind are the cultivation of the olive and the vine, and the bullfight. Things are mostly done in a slapdash way as if they were not really worth doing at all, including those that actually mean a great deal. In the great religious feasts of Holy Week or Corpus Christi decorations are left half done, triumphal processions start late, go either too fast or too slow until hitches and hold-ups occur one after the other, the robes of the clergy may be soiled or crumpled and dignitaries and soldiers will slouch along at their own sweet will. Anyone used to the faultless timing and perfect detail, the balance between imaginative display and mechanical precision, of a Royal drive through London might assume that Spaniards did not take such matters seriously. And everything manufactured there falls quickly apart, as if to remind us of the impermanence of the world itself: everything, that is to say, but what of its nature and function ought to do so, for much time may pass in the struggle to free tomato paste or anchovies from their tin or drinks from their bottle. It is not that Spaniards are incapable of efficiency or even really indifferent to it, but they apparently do not desire it enough to make the effort to achieve it: to do so, no doubt, would leave them with less time for real life.

And in spite of all that Gibraltar had to offer it was with a profound thankfulness and sense of home-going that I would pass the neat polite security officers under their spruce Union Jack and cross the No Man's Land to where small nonchalant men in need of a shave and a new uniform waited to give their perfunctory inspection. A visit to Gibraltar heightened the appreciation of Spain by simply interrupting it, somewhat as we relish a good night's sleep all the better for waking now and then. And always on the return trip to Arroyo de la Miel, as the coach bounced over pits in the road left yawning there since the last heavy rains and past neon signs with half the letters failing to light until, by a pardonable error, the driver drew up a mile or so beyond my stop and smilingly wished me a safe walk home: and as I trudged through the darkness to where Puri, purged and exalted, would be waiting with a simple yet hideous meal, I would muse on the gaps in the Spanish composition and on the fact that they did not in the least matter: on the fact, indeed, that it would be a black day were Spaniards ever to change, in this respect or that or the other.

❧ 4 ❧

IN THIS MANNER THE DAYS AND WEEKS SPED BY. THE
Judas Tree, in Andalusia known as the Tree of Love, burst
into showers of purple blossom that crawled and buzzed with
bees. Through the open doors of the peasant dwellings down
the road came the merry piping of newly-hatched chickens.
Little round white buds had set among the dark pointed leaves
of the oranges and lemons. The consequential burping of
frogs arose in the dykes round the plantings of sugar-cane and
cicadas twanged in the whiskery foliage above. Great black or
yellow oxen, yoked in pairs and grave-eyed under the frivolous
red bobbles of their headgear, dragged their light wooden
ploughs in and out of the olive trees. Then scarlet flowers
appeared one day on the thorny pomegranate bushes in the
garden. The pomegranate is a late-comer: now it was time to
go.

Shopping and householding had filled out my vocabulary
and showed me a little of the way that Andalusia manages her
affairs. I had learned a thing or two about the Andalusian mind,
although I felt further and further away from understanding it,
as will often happen with increased familiarity. These strange
people and their customs were a favourite theme with an
acquaintance from the north, a scholar and author who was
also farming and building in the region. To begin with, he
said, it was impossible to know them until you had employed
them a long while and in quantity. This sounded reasonable
enough, but I was never quite persuaded. New aspects of their
character would naturally appear in your daily attenuating

43

battle with them to get things done, but they might not be such very important aspects. Andalusians do not look on time spent thus as the important part of the day, contempt for sordid activity having come down to them with the rest of the Islamic heritage.

Listening to the brilliant talk of the man from the north I used to wonder if one could never know a country not one's own or if, on the contrary, one had to be an outsider to know a country at all. He saw any amount of light and shade while seeming to overlook the outlines. "Here, when they do you down, they get angry with you as well," he once declared, shaking with laughter. "If you see a man turn away and spit as you come along, you can be sure that he is stealing from you." This was true, but it had struck me time and again in other parts of Spain, including his own, and indeed in other parts of the world. But although he knew his country and the world much better than I did, it was for some reason only here that this peculiarity had attracted his attention.

He was greatly amused also at the self-sufficiency of the local people, even of those who were well educated. They believed, he declared, that Malaga was the core of the universe and that all beyond was darkness and confusion. Now and again he would make the journey to town to meet an assortment of intellectuals in a *tertulia* and invariably was staggered by their lack of interest in anything outside their own circle. It is indeed remarkable and Gerald Brenan has a story to illustrate it. He is a keen botanist and fell in with a Malaga man who shared this hobby. Together they roamed the Sierras to the north of the city in pursuit of the beautiful or rare and once Brenan called out to his companion to come quickly and look at a plant which was both; but this he would not do, for it was some twelve metres over the boundary line and within the province of Granada and hence no possible concern of his. However, we must walk before we run and it is unusual to find an Andalusian with any interest in plant life at all beyond its

44

culinary use. In the Sierra de Ronda lives the fir tree known as *pin sapo* which once covered Europe, was then gradually pushed southward in the Ice Age and can now be found nowhere else in the world. There is no need to go scrambling over the rocks in search of it because a few have been planted in the little *plaza* in the heart of Ronda itself which overlooks the gorge and the mountain range. But I have yet to come across a local man who cares whether the *pin sapo* survives in his area or not, and Spaniards in Ronda as a rule are engaged either in peering down into the abyss or striking an attitude in front of a camera.

Again, this indifference to all that does not directly and practically concern oneself is to be found all over Spain. Just as Jews have been described as like other human beings only more so, we might define the Andalusians as Spaniards who are particularly Spanish.

They have an intense passionate interest in other people that is most endearing, and a whole world away from the elaborate French shrug. It bubbles perennially in the Andalusian heart and is love of life itself. The old peasant by the well puts her heavy jar aside to ask if the stranger is married and if God has given children: it is the fundamentals that she wishes to hear about and the smart city man sitting opposite you in the train is no less eager for information, even though more sophisticated in approach. Eyes follow the newcomer up the street from behind pulled shutters, eyes that may be critical, hostile or sardonic but never indifferent: clever tongues will give him a nickname, one very likely chosen all too well.

Maria, wife of the Antonio who had a fruit, vegetable and provision store in San Miguel, was a true Andaluza. I listened one day with delight as she harangued a Dutchman rash enough to assert that *chirimoyas*, or custard pears, were not the delectable fruit that Spaniards pretended. He went so far as to say that the sweet insipid flesh of it did nothing to compensate him for the number of big black wooden pips. For Maria no

45

two opinions on this, or any other, subject were admissible. She held the scaly green object between finger and thumb and bent forward over the marble counter as the words poured out, she threw herself heart and soul into the struggle to convince him of his error before it could get a grip on him and cast a shadow over his life. But all at once, just outside her shop as if pre-arranged, a motor-car ran into a boy on a cycle and he fell to the ground, badly hurt. There was blood in plenty on the cobbles, *sangre*, that marvel, that precious thing that no self-respecting Spaniard can see without emotion. Her lips shaped by the last word she uttered, the *chirimoya* still poised in the air, Maria froze to a statue which none the less quivered from head to foot with expectancy. Dutchman, store, husband and children were forgotten completely: nothing in the world existed but *la suerte* made manifest at her door. The foreigner spoke, she did not hear. He played with her, crying that a thief had run off with a bunch of bananas, that he could smell something burning in her kitchen, that poor Antonio was being marched away at that very moment by two police. He might as well have been talking to the alabaster goddess on a fountain. To see Maria then was to grasp fully the meaning of the phrase "to be all eyes".

My thoughts turned ruefully back to the days when I would stand all night to get into the Russian Ballet or travel across all Europe in a wooden railway carriage. Spanish vitality can make one feel very old.

Whenever I think of Andalusia episodes come to mind in this way, like shots from a film. The land projects itself in a series of images as if it were only to be apprehended through the eye: a coat of arms on a crumbling wall in a dying village, a flood of scarlet geranium pouring down a snowy façade, a train-load of young soldiers in shabby uniforms, storks perched high on the bell-towers of churches, lemons hanging on a tree against a brilliant sky, an old beggar asleep in the shade of a doorway, the lanterns of fishing boats as they dip and sway above the sea at night. The people likewise manifest themselves in scenes, as if taking part in an immense charade.

There was the afternoon that Pepe lost his temper, which was very much like the end of the world. He had a gentle muffin face on which an amiable smile was fixed as steadily as the beret on his head, and nothing ever seemed to ruffle or vex him. One of the itinerant madmen of Malaga opened the door of his bar one time and flung in a sackful of fruit skins and vegetable peels, whereat Pepe gave a little shrug, indicating that after all it took many sorts to make a world. Thirsty foreign sailors who drank themselves on to the floor he took in his stride, nor did he ever do more than just glance up when a picket removed the bodies. Thus to find him one afternoon wearing a foreign naval cap in place of his beret did not astonish: it was an un-Spanish kind of thing to do and yet somehow in harmony with his view of life. His beret meanwhile was on the sailor's head. The sailor kept pointing to the advertisement for Coca-Cola, that *escudo* of the free world, and bawling "amigo! amigo!" Then he reached over and took the bottle of Fundador and poured out a glass for himself, while Pepe smiled. He seized a handful of *tapas* and gulped them down. Next he violently shook hands with Pepe and moved round the bar to embrace him, capsizing the brandy bottle. The smile on Pepe's face as he yielded to that ursine hug was calm and unmoved and indifferent as the smile of a buddhist deity. All continued in peace and love until the naval hero blundered up to the till and began playfully to ring up sales, whereat Pepe was instantly and alarmingly transformed. His shouts gradually penetrated even that whirling brain until the poor wight hastily recovered his cap and stumbled away into the baking afternoon sun. Pepe went shouting on, quite unable to stop even while he bade us welcome and asked what we would have. When he had served us he went to the door and notified the street in a stentorian voice of what had just taken place. His emotions were similar to, although probably stronger than, those of a witness to the desecration of an altar.

I remember another scene in another bar, an obscure bar in Seville. It was in the form of a horseshoe and the upper half of a man was seen across it, every inch of it conveying a tremendous emotion. The eyes burned with fury, the skin was white, the mouth rigid with disdain, the very sit of the head on the shoulders expressive of illimitable, ineffable contempt. Beside him were foreigners again, productive of so much trouble: they were talking a language he understood and criticizing Spain. They were people of no manners or morals, pariahs, base born, to eat her bread and mock her thus. They were of the low sort who would stay in a man's house as honoured guests and then make off with the silver. The nostrils dilated like those of a mettlesome horse, the chest heaved, it seemed that a duel must follow. For what they were saying was true.

Here, then, was the proverbial Spanish pride, another offshoot of Spanish vitality and like no other pride in the world. It was the superb, ridiculous face of *hidalguía* and willy-nilly one had to admire it. This pride was a thing so beautiful in itself that the fact of its being misplaced, as dull or academic minds might judge it to be, was neither here nor there. With all one's heart one wished the strangers to pay for their drinks and go away, but they went on laughing and talking, oblivious and impervious.

The *hidalgo* threw a five-peseta coin on the bar and, in the disturbed condition of his mind, never picked up the fifty cents change. Still the foreigners did not turn their heads. He flung his cloak about him and stalked off and now at last they took delighted notice, for his action had, as it were, completely altered the skyline. The *hidalgo* was now eight or nine inches shorter: all this while he had been perching on the footrail that ran round the bar, hooked securely in position by the heels of his Andalusian boots. His spiritual grandeur, however, was not affected – if anything was increased – by the strangers'

48

mirth and again he carried one with him. No peacock in full pride ever strutted like this noble bantam as he left surroundings so unworthy: as he went he seemed to pass under innumerable phantom arches while a phantom guitar played and a nasal voice sang, melancholy and indomitable, a tune coming from far away over arid plains and snow-capped mountains.

These people are more completely themselves, more absolutely of a piece than any I know. Recently I walked down the main street of an Andalusian village during a spell of most untypical weather, when the puddles and drains were frozen stiff and the leaves hung down limp and brown with cold. Men in broad hats and short coats with ragged fur collars were sitting in front of their houses or round the café in the square, shivering and blue in the face. Sunday morning mass had just concluded and it was their custom to sit in the open at this hour, a custom that they did not propose to change merely because of a bitter frost. From an evolutionary point of view this bullish fixity of mind may not altogether make sense, but it undoubtedly gives Spain a part of her special flavour.

❧ 5 ❧

THERE IS A KIND OF MANIAC WHO MUST TEASE HIMSELF
with problems that are practically certain not to arise: whom to
choose as a fellow castaway on a desert island, perhaps, or
whether he would prefer to marry George Eliot or George
Sand. Both matters would be child's play compared with the
choosing of one Spanish city to be lived in or visited to the
exclusion of all others. A tourist after six weeks in the country,
rolling in a comfortable car from place to place, might see no
difficulty in it for the hazy impressions he had received would
be likely to result in some clear preference. If he got to Santiago
de Compostela on one of the cloudless days of the Galician
summer he would carry away an exquisite memory of grey
stone and green leaf swimming in a gentle mysterious light far
removed from the harsh brilliance of the south. But if he did
not, if he decided to dally among the fleshpots of La Coruña
or the drowsy charms of Pontevedra and so arrive the following day in heavy rain, he would remember a confusion of mud
and steaming oxen, dripping roofs, plain women carrying
heavy burdens on their heads, doleful faces peering from
archways and chubby priests lifting their skirts as they skipped
over the puddles. He might get to Madrid for the *fiesta* of San
Isidro in May when that austere grey city is hung with crimson
and yellow tapestries and adorned with banks of flowers, and
Castilian sobriety gives place to wine and song. He might strike
Granada from the list altogether on account of some disagreeable experience in the gipsy caves of Sacromonte: he might see
Bilbao in rather too rosy a light for the excellence of its food.

Once we become familiar with the great cities of Spain, each with its strong and even violent personality, each splendid in a different way, the choice of a favourite seems impossible. I do, however, own to an old peculiar and ever increasing affection for Malaga. Other cities are more handsome or more lively, richer in historical monuments or treasures of art, and set in equally beautiful surroundings. No great cultural life flourishes there, but the same is true of many other cities, the streams of Spanish life running too deep and too narrow for such diffusions of energy: and it need not worry us because quite soon in that balmy air we shall unregretfully cease to look for it. But the various lacks and shortcomings somehow add to the charm and we can love a place as we love a human being all the better for not knowing exactly why.

Malaga's history is varied and turbulent like that of most Spanish cities, and particularly of those on the Mediterranean seaboard. Founded by the Phoenicians, at one time or another it was ruled by Carthage, Rome, the Visigoths and the Moors, fretted by the pirates of Barbary and ravaged by the troops of Napoleon. Ferdinand and Isabella freed it from Islam in 1487 and in celebration granted it a coat of arms in 1494, with the two young martyr-saints of Roman times, Ciriaco and Paula, standing each on a tower of the Gibralfaro, a splendid old castle on the hill which is thought to be Greek in origin although the crumbling walls we see are Moorish: then, a foreground of waves in honour of the port, a bordering device of bows and arrows and a ducal crown capping the whole. Thereafter adjectives were bestowed on the town from time to time, as badges are on boy scouts. In 1640 Philip IV awarded the description *Very Noble* and *Very Loyal* as a reward for its attitude in the war with Portugal. After Malaga declared in 1843 against the Regency and for the Constitution, Isabella II conceded a further *Very Illustrious, Always Intrepid* and *Foremost in Freedom's Peril.* For its conduct when the German battleship *Gneisenau* was wrecked and sunk in 1900 it was given a

Very Hospitable; and with Don Alfonso XIII's *Very Beneficent*, commemorating its help to sick or wounded soldiers back from Morocco, it was fully made up. During the Civil War it was at first in the hands of the republicans, who burned a good many churches, monasteries and convents, and then in those of the nationalists, who shot an inordinate number of people.

The best place to see it is from the Gibralfaro. You climb up to the summit by steep narrow twisting paths with lizards darting into the scrub every time you put down a foot, and the city lies below laid out like a model. The bull-ring seems disproportionately big and the cathedral rather small. Stone jetties embrace the harbour like the claws of a crab. The Roman theatre which is one of the oldest monuments appears to be one of the newest because it is only within the last few years that the excavations were completed. Now and then when the wind is favourable to it a plume of smoke from the cement works to the north obscures the entire prospect; and on a clear day there is an incomparable view of the Penibetica range, so rounded and crumpled with age it appears to have been pinched out of soft clay by a giant finger and thumb. Behind this again are the harder stronger peaks of the Sierras, some of them covered in snow.

It is also a pleasure to come in from the sea. The port is a friendly ramshackle one and looks sizeable enough in the ordinary way, with Spanish naval craft, coastal steamers, trawlers and yachts riding within the stone *muelles*. But now and then an American warship enters and scales it all down to a sort of toy. Indeed, the whole city appears to shrink as hundreds of giants descend on it, pouring into the shops, being taken in the fullest sense for rides by the waterfront jarveys and sleeping in the bars and taverns, their caps drowsily nodding like so many huge snowdrops.

I never knew Malaga before the Civil War and so cannot repine for what I have not seen. Larios must have been very fine with its old patrician houses and their massive doors and well-proportioned windows before it was shelled and burned. But some of the townspeople regard the shiny front of plate-glass and the array of merchandise as a case of good coming out of evil. I did know the charming little square at the upper end before they put in the abominable fountain that everyone seems to be proud of. It is melancholy to reflect on the sum that must have been swallowed up by that eyesore, with its outrageous form and vile colour, the colour of some virulent, factory-made *crême de menthe*. We must hope that no one will be rich enough or evil enough to improve the honeycomb of little old streets all round the square. Already, flushed with prosperity, madmen are tearing up the old paving-stones and cobbles and laying there instead a kind of marble tile which, at the first fall of rain, becomes as slippery as ice. A number of the good old shabby cafés have quietly closed their doors, to make way for cafeterias and supermarkets.

An English resident who worries a good deal about what other people say used to reprove me for driving about in the hackney carriages. He considered it appropriate only for tourists, a baffling idea as I thought, because a tourist could find little pleasure in jogging slowly and in silence under the trees of the Alameda and round the villas, pensions and clinics of prosaic Limonar. It is necessary to go uphill to find the beautiful places and the drivers are not going to wear their horses out or sharpen their appetites if they can help it. The whole fun of the thing is the driver himself and what he has to say. His race is a gloomy one on the whole, with a vein of puckish fancy that comes out only now and then, usually in discussion about the fare. It joins with Adolf Hitler in believing that lies stand a better chance when they are thumping big ones. "Look at my horse, Señora!" they cry, indicating the bag of skin and bone that waits with piteously drooping head between the shafts, "you have no idea how much corn he eats." Or, "Too much, Señora? Do you know why I make you this special price? Because you are a lady and I am a caballero."

Unlike Hitler, on the other hand, they are disarming and engaging and apt to get their wicked way in the end. Their silences can be as effective as their speech: watch them spit as the military governor sweeps by in a car the size of a small house, note the derision in every line of head, shoulder and back as a *Guardia* on point duty curses them. You are recalled at once to the great days of the silent film. And one afternoon as we demurely trotted past the bull-ring a lorry flew out of a side turning and all but carried off a wheel, at which both horse and driver were swept by a kind of noble frenzy and, dead to police, oblivious of tram and car, regardless of self and encouraged by the shouts of an equally noble public, gave chase in the best tradition of Ben Hur until finally the wheel came off and bowled away and we fell in a tangled heap by the road. There was no ignoble whining about the damage, still less any womanish concern for the passenger: the little gnome with the bad breath and the cast in his eye was treading on air, as Andalusians do when they feel they have risen to an occasion.

It is odd how from all the incidents and encounters of daily life memory picks out this or that one, apparently of no more interest than others it lets go. That I should remember the coachman is not surprising because it is rare nowadays to be thrown from a horse-drawn vehicle. Another, less accountable, recollection I have is of the *callista* who works somewhere behind the cathedral, near the little garden with the orange trees and the bishop's palace with the enchanting baroque façade. *Callistas* are chiropodists and in no other part of the world do I take up more than ten minutes of their time. This young and pretty woman with the dyed copper hair spent an hour and three-quarters at it, working methodically but at a snail's pace and breaking off now and again to yawn like a tiger. Towards the end of the session, yawning compulsively myself, I remarked that she seemed to be weary and she answered, no, she was not weary at all, she was bored. *Aburrida,* she said, and the very word was like a chain round the neck. And now whenever I pass that way I think of her up there, languidly plying her tools, languidly laying them down to give herself up the more completely and voluptuously to her yawn, fixed in boredom like a fly in treacle with the clock in the cathedral tower relentlessly booming the hours away over her window.

That little quarter of old narrow streets and the other one beyond Larios are the best places imaginable for *flânerie*: the French word has to be used, there is no help for it, even "stroll" is faintly tinged with Anglo-Saxon purposefulness. There are rows of shops to stare at, with hunters' jack-knives in the window, or great iron pans for cooking *paella*, exquisite gold and silver work, strings of rosaries, baskets woven of rush or twig, plaster saints, gay coarse pottery from Granada and Talavera; and old-world apothecaries with pestles and mortars, herbal jars, marble counters and huge glass vats of red and green, offering every imaginable patent medicine *Elaborado en Barcelona* for sale. Here and there is a cheap wine bar, a monastic haunt of wooden barrels, wooden tables and chairs and sawdust strewn about the floor: it is severe and decent, with no frills or decoration apart from the bull-fight posters on the wall, and it is no place at all for women.

As the years went by this charming old part became extremely familiar, as my dressmaker lived there and I never could find her house. She had no business card and was not in the telephone book and when after an hour or so of perambulation I would fall on the building with the brass plates calling attention to the *partera* or midwife and the *clínico* for *rayos X* that also occupied it I would be too relieved and happy to think of noting the address. The dressmaker was short and immensely fat, with a large cool mind: she wore the pronounced moustache which is supposedly attractive in Spanish women and like all her kind dressed only when she was going out. I do not recollect that she ever took measurements or used a pattern, and the creations that lay in heaps about her small dark room were not at all good. Either she was ignorant of this fact or indifferent to it, for she described all she did as *muy bonito* and her client as *muy guapa* as long as the garment was on. Criticism or suggestion she could not abide and at the first chilling breath of it would turn to stone until all blew over. To this day I cannot fix her whereabouts more exactly than as somewhere behind the Teatro Cervantes. Everyone, even a Malagueño, knows the little Teatro because most of the time it serves as a cinema. It once was my privilege there to see an English war film dubbed with Spanish voices, wild torrents of speech bursting from stiff upper lips with amazing effect.

But there too I saw the great Antonio during the first season in Malaga that he ever gave, although not unhappily on the first night when the audience went wild. He came before the curtain on that occasion and, like a good Spaniard, declared that he owed everything to his mother, whereupon a spotlight rested on a comfortable person in mink who wept, and Antonio wept, and the audience wept, and a capital time was had by all. He danced superbly as ever the evening I saw him, rhythm and time so perfect that music and dance seemed as one and the same thing; but his waist was beginning ever so little to thicken. Life is short and art is long and cruel as it is, often by the time a dancer has technical mastery he is growing fat: his decline begins at the period when painters and writers and musicians are looking forward to their best years. A male Spanish dancer needs a body as straight and thin as a young tree and no amount of experience, temperament or technique can make up for its loss: above all it expresses sexual passion, a fire between man and woman, and the merest hint of middle-age has an effect of indecency. None the less, Antonio had lost nothing of speed or agility and he streaked about the stage like summer lightning: indeed, the look he gave one of the troupe who collided with him might have blasted an oak. He had with him a partner better than any I had seen except the captivating Rosario. This girl was very young, slender and beautiful, and repeatedly crossed herself and murmured

56

prayers as she waited in the wings for the moment to come; and then, a new creature all at once, she took the stage, the embodiment of pride and haughty assurance and dancing with such perfection that a man beside me groaned with delight as an old dog does when his ears are fondled. They were all dancing like angels that night, the understanding as well as the love and admiration of the public passing to them and acting as galvanizer. Sympathy is essential to *flamenco* singers and dancers, great or small. I have seen Antonio dance in Dublin one rainy afternoon to a phlegmatic crowd without the glimmer of an idea as to what he was doing and which only came alive when the company did some crude but vigorous Galician folk-trot reminiscent of a jig. One would hardly have known it was he, except for the gipsy glances shooting here and there like a serpent's tongue. This evening he was on the heights, however, and was called to curtain after curtain until at last the final one came down and no amount of calling and clapping, even that peculiar thunderous clapping of Spain, could persuade it to rise: and in the deep contentment, the sense of being spiritually full fed, that such great performances leave behind them we went away into a starlit night and into Garrido's, the gay but homely café that might have been the model for Hemingway's *Clean Well-lighted Place*.

❧ 6 ❧

SPRING IN ANDALUSIA IS A GOOD TIME TO TRAVEL. THE
Japanese say the four terrors of life are earthquake, fire, flood,
and father, and where Spain is concerned I would add,
foreigners and fiestas. By foreigners, naturally, I do not mean
myself. I mean the Gothic hordes in search of wine and sun
and cheap living who take no interest in the land or its people
and have no respect for *costumbre*. There are the grisly patches
of them all the year round along the Costa del Sol described
above, but on the whole they are an affliction of the summer,
like wasps in the wine. And fiestas, apart from beginning much
later than they should and going on too long, tend to obscure
the wonder and beauty of Spain, which is ordinary workaday
life.

April or March are the best months for visiting Cordoba.
Winter there is colder than in Malaga and summer hotter,
and both are to be avoided. The Cordoba spring is mild and
the city is never crowded then except in Holy Week. A TAF
leaves Malaga at noon three times a week and arrives about
4 p.m.

On a sunny spring day it is the most delightful journey
imaginable. The *vega* beyond Malaga then is bright with
yellow oxalis, which is a native of Africa and brought over the
sea in cargoes of grain, and Stars of the Virgin, a charming
little flower like the common daisy. A green mist goes creeping
up the boughs of the poplars and silver birches and the air
smells of lemon and aromatic herbs. The Sierras keep their
winter hat of snow from which an icy little wind shoots down

now and then, to the despair of buds and butterflies and Anglo-Saxons lying on the beach. Many of the white farmhouses are built on the tops of steep hills, as if their owners were determined to make their lives as hard as possible. In this region doors and windows are often painted blue, in the hope of scaring evil spirits away.

Presently the train comes to the Hoyo del Chorro, a reservoir built for the electrification and irrigation of the Malaga area, and a truly marvellous sight. Fifteen tunnels have been cut through the masses of rock and between them one may sometimes catch sight of the gorges and ravines, or the magnificent leaping red cliffs far overhead and the eagles hovering and circling over the peaks. Round and about those mighty crags there winds a path with a handrail which visitors are not allowed to use, although needless to say they do so. It is possible to stand there and peer into the gulf with the eagles sweeping and wheeling below, listening to the whish! and whoof! of their mighty wings.

After El Chorro the country grows wilder and sterner. Mountains appear in all manner of weird and ill-assorted shapes, as if to impress on the stranger that they are before anything else Spanish and individualist. All at once a single peak towers irrelevantly on the horizon like a pyramid: then comes a mountain that is the very image of a whale floating on the surface of the ocean: another has a great double limestone ridge thrown about it, like a city protected by two walls instead of one. And there are fields of young corn, fiery green, the surface dimpled by the wind to look like rushing water till you could swear it was a river and the fall not far away. Flocks of goats abound, the kids skipping round their mothers as merry as puppies. The pruned vines stick up out of the pink or red clay like a multitude of black rams' horns. Everywhere is the glorious olive, the silvery feathery branches waving gently in the breeze, each separate tree standing in its own little pool of lilac shade. The groves on the distant hillsides look like dark stripes on a pink waistcoat.

At the junction of Bobadilla the TAF pauses for lunch. Bobadilla as the spider's web of Andalusia is associated in the experienced mind with endless periods of waiting, with fear, doubt, introspection and hence misery and feelings of guilt. We cannot think how we come to be there unless indeed we deserve it. But on this unique journey Bobadilla is where a full Spanish luncheon has to be eaten in twenty-five minutes. It is served in a dingy room with an early Victorian iron stove plumb in the middle and dusty mirrors round the walls. A pipe carries the smoke of the stove away through the roof and half-way up this pipe, astonishingly, is a cluster of four iron lanterns. Rows and rows of wine bottles and coarse earthenware plates with green and orange figures are the only other ornament.

The waiter regards it as a matter of personal honour to see that you receive every mouthful of your entitlement under the fixed-price tariff. As soon as the travellers are seated he places before them a helping of *arroz*, cool sticky and bright yellow, a single misleading shrimp on the summit and a few sandy *almejas* or clams within. Doubling like a hare, he tracks to the kitchen and reappears to engage almost literally in an egg-and-spoon race: for each of the plates balanced on his arms holds two eggs, fried in the inimitable Spanish style so that they manage to be frothy and rubbery at once, swimming in a carmine lake of tomato sauce. These, with ancient Mediterranean skill, he deals out, flick-flick, like so many cards, and runs to the kitchen again. Every time the door is opened we may enjoy a waft of hot olive oil and the roars of the cook. Back he bustles, with plates of fried fish and watery green salad. To the kitchen once more and out, with *chuletas de ternera*, or veal chops. Some of his steadily munching clients are only halfway through their eggs, and he shakes his head at them and points to the clock. Some of us even attempt to refuse a course, but nothing comes of it. Yet again he flies to the kitchen and emerges with *flan* for all. After that he streaks round the tables collecting the money. By now the TAF is giving mournful cries like some great wounded animal and we run to it, while the waiter stands back exhausted but triumphant, tapping his watch and exclaiming "Eso es! eso es! eso es!"

Soon the countryside changes completely again. We have come to the valley of the Guadalquivir, a tongue of green licking up through the brown and grey Sierras from the sea to Linares. There is nothing now but undulating slopes of a soft vivid green, wide luminous skies and tranquil ponds reflecting them. The ancient town of Montilla is the last place of interest before we reach our destination. A Roman foundation, it was later the birthplace of Gonzalve Fernández de Córdoba, or *El Gran Capitán* as he is always known, conqueror of Naples and enemy of the *preux* Bayard, who lived from 1443 to 1515 and was one of the finest soldiers Spain ever had. There are the neglected remains of an Arab stronghold overthrown in 1508 by Charles V, the Emperor of the West. But the real claim of Montilla to our reverence, and our gratitude, is the wine she produces, from vines scattered all over the two hills on which she is standing. This wine is the colour of good honey, with something of its fragrance: it is full enough but never gross, sharp and sweet at once but never harsh or insipid, it would be a wine of European stature if only it travelled well. But unhappily it does not and there is even a saying that it should not be taken across a river. So, if we are travelling northward, Cordoba will be the last point where it may rightly be enjoyed and we should see that this is done. Both piety and commonsense demand it, for *in partibus infidelium* it becomes something else altogether and the wines known as *amontillados* give no idea of it at all.

Presently the TAF slides into Cordoba station. Although it is hardly late at all by meridional standards, the taxi-drivers are fast asleep to a man as if they had given up hope of ever seeing

61

it. Not so very long ago a crowd of ragged cabbies and hotel touts would have besieged the traveller the instant he climbed from the train, shrieking at him and pulling his clothes; which makes the present state of affairs all the more remarkable. And not only are the drivers all fast asleep but it vexes them to be woken up. They frown and yawn and put their caps on their oily heads with leaden hands. But there is no help for it, the station is on the very tip of the town and the travellers are not going to walk. So they resign themselves, even in time grow cheerful, as the taxis rattle away down the broad new avenues or ancient twisty lanes, with rows of dusty oranges along them still covered with dusty fruit, to the various hotels, *pensions* and *hospedajes* of the town.

> *¡Oh siempre gloriosa patria mia,*
> *Tanto por plumas cuanto por espadas!*

These are two of fourteen ecstatic lines addressed to Cordoba by the great Andaluz poet Luis de Góngora y Argote, who lived much of his life in the city and died there in 1627. They are inscribed on a roll of marble facing the Roman bridge, immediately in front of the Triumph of the Archangel Raphael, an extravagant memorial I have long preferred to a great many works of superior merit. The pedestal of rock includes some palm trees writhing as if in a tornado and a plump lady or two, and from it springs up a marble pillar with San Raphael in gilt perched on top and surveying the city he protects. The effect produced is very much like that of a bolting lettuce. In front a headless nymph rides on a dolphin, a creature dear to Spanish fancy: her head rolls about in the dust near by. Nettles and other wild flora grow freely in the crevices of this masterpiece, while behind it and above it are the magnificent warm yellow walls of the Grand Mosque.

Cordoba does not change, even if it does a little decay. Those narrow lanes where the houses lean towards each other and geraniums tumble from the windows in a rosy flood, where through massive Arab doorways you catch the sparkle of a fountain in a shady courtyard, have altered little since Góngora walked in them four hundred years ago. And how he belonged there, what an Andalusian he was! Gay, pleasure-mad, fond of women and horses, addicted to bull-fighting and gambling, and yet a clerk in holy orders: in his poetry sensitive and tender, melancholy and ironic by turns, in life a pepperpot who laced into all who annoyed him with a pen that stung like a cobra. It was the habit then for poets of differing schools to attack each other with the asperity of Early Fathers arguing insignificant points of doctrine, a habit resulting from the ardent desire for cohesion and conformity that we find running through all Spanish history side by side with an equally passionate longing for the opposite. The literary scene was strewn with corpses, so to speak, with the Holy Office ever at hand to ban the works of survivors.

The nobleman Góngora experienced fame and loneliness, poverty and riches, love and sorrow, before he died. He had no vocation for the priesthood and did not allow his clerical status to restrict his way of life. He mingled with the wealthy and great in Madrid and with the peasants of his own region. He met El Greco and admired him, and wrote a verse later on his tomb. His poetry often breathes the very spirit of the Andalusian countryside and calls up thoughts of herds and flocks pouring over parched yellow ground or between dark ilex trees, shepherds sitting round a fire in darkness, the Guadalquivir placidly mirroring a fiery evening sky, wind ruffling silky grey olive boughs, the flight of cranes, the leaping of horses. In *The Literature of the Spanish People* Mr Brenan makes particular reference to Góngora's exact observation of nature, giving as example the youth sleeping out with shepherds and kept awake all night by their dogs barking at the rustle of the dry oak leaves.

I remember a delightful experience with a friend, searching

for the house where Góngora had worked and died. It is always pleasant to have a definite aim although there was no hurry about it: in places with a strong Eastern flavour like this one time always seems more plentiful than in others. We wandered about the town, renewing acquaintance with old sights and sounds, finding all the same as ever. In Judios we went into the old synagogue, a mere hole in the wall but a very impressive one with its dusty slabs and old gallery and its sense of a vanished life. An aged Jew, so old he might almost have been the last Rabbi to expound the law there, slowly and toothlessly mumbled over each of the stones in his care, in a lingo which he apparently believed to be English. I wondered how many weeks more he could possibly last, and my friend told me she had passed that way ten years before and wondered the same thing then.

On to El Potro, where the little horse so gaily surmounts the fountain splashing below him, and to El Cristo de los Dolores, hanging in a bower of iron street-lamps. We passed a house with a plaque on the wall carrying a single word: Manolete. If a philosopher had been born there, a Nobel prize-winner, a renowned doctor or scholar, some details would have been necessary; but not for a great bull-fighter.

Presently, however, we began the search in a business-like manner. We had been told that the house was somewhere in the Plaza Mayor, but citizens when appealed to told us there was no such place. Plaza Mayor? *No hay*. A little group collected round us and soon worked it out that we meant the Plaza Antigua. We carefully followed their instructions and at last came on a square which was, after all, named the Plaza Mayor. Here a closed market, obviously built at great expense and occupying more or less the whole available space to the exclusion of light and air from all surrounding houses, was being dismantled stone by stone. One of the workmen had been injured by falling masonry, and an ambulance had arrived to take him away. There was no sense to be got from

64

the crowd, who stood around mesmerized by the hope of seeing blood. The police were frantic with the strain of guiding the ambulance to the spot and getting it away afterwards. To put our query to them would have invited summary arrest. We marched about the square with stones dropping on us, as in an air raid, until finally we recognized that our information was false.

Then we had a good idea. A bookshop, focal point of culture, would tell us what we wanted to know. We would buy a map or a few postcards, make a little polite conversation and then raise our problem. Our hearts leaped up at the thought that we should now be on the right track within a few moments; but we were wrong. Not only had the bookseller no idea at all of Góngora's birthplace but we caused him a hideous embarrassment. He had too much integrity to send us away with the first direction that entered his head, as many people would; but to confess to ignorance filled his heart with death. But then he, in turn, had a good idea and ran to the telephone. He rang the local luminaries one after the other, but none of them could help in the slightest. Then a shabby little gnome, browsing in a book that he plainly never intended to buy, looked up and said that it was, of course, in the Plaza de las Bulas. That *plaza*, when we found it, proved to be the one we had passed through several times already. It had been re-named Plaza Maimónides, in the mistaken belief that the great Cordoban Jewish doctor, philosopher and theologian of the twelfth century was born in one of the houses there. The house of the alleged birth was now the Museo Municipal, although no one called it that. It was known to the populace as the Museo Taurino and was chiefly devoted to Manolete.

This was, I now saw, to be exactly like every other search of its kind in the south of Spain. All were desirous, none was capable, of helping us to our goal, modest as it might seem. Policemen were getting to know us by sight and hurriedly turning away as time and again we entered the field of their vision. In the Museo Taurino a young man with the blue-black hair of the true gipsy told us to go to the Calle Jesús-Maria and look for the Cine Góngora, because the poet's birthplace was next door at No. 17. That was how the cinema came by its name. As our hopes receded our determination grew, and although we could no longer remember why we wished to see this particular house at all we set off again at a brisk pace. The young man's statement proved to have been mere improvisation. Undoubtedly there was a Cine Góngora, but no mention of the poet himself anywhere in the street. A kindly passer-by came up, however, and gave us very precise instructions indeed as to where we could find his house; and these we assiduously followed, ending up once more outside the Museo Taurino.

The young man with the raven hair smiled at us, as one who had been quietly waiting for something just like this to happen. He said and, broken at last, we agreed, that it would be better to abandon the search now and look at the museum. There was silver work and painting as well as the bull-fighting relics, although not a very great deal. He spoke in Spanish, a point in his favour, but even for a Cordoban guide was weak in his information. Among other caprices, he would have it that various pictures of Christ with the Crown of Thorns were old Arab paintings. Argument he disposed of by pretending not to hear it, and it was evident that his spiritual armour left no chink for the entry of any self-questioning at all.

The taurine display contrived to be intensely moving and faintly absurd at once. Manolete's death-mask was of a lean and dedicated melancholy face, the poet's face that great *toreros* often have, wearing a closed sardonic look as if he savoured a grim but private jest. From the photographs hanging all round, it appeared that this look was never far away, in moments of triumph as of suspense or peril: the man seemed always meditating something beyond the horizons of the crowd, a bitter something that was no mere premonition of death in the ring. The hide of the great bull that killed him

66

was stretched over an entire wall of one room. Then the grimy underwear of other fighters was laid out, with holes in it where horns had gone in: there were capes by the dozen, all embroidered by hand, more often than not the work of nuns; and *trajes de luces*, more photographs, more death-masks. Round the walls were the mounted heads of bulls, staring down at the room with the fixed and unswerving stupidity for which another and kinder word is *nobleza*. It is fine to be noble and it is also fine to be alive: we all of course prefer the former state but the ripe wisdom of Falstaff's homily on that theme must find an echo in many hearts. And if bulls were only cute enough, or base enough, to ignore the cape and attack the man the fight would be over at once.

Next in value to the Manolete relics, as the guide saw it, was an artificial moon installed in the patio: indeed, as he spoke of it, he was quite carried away.

The house itself was harmoniously proportioned, combining strength with delicacy and suggesting a life of dignity, taste and minimal labour. On every visit to Cordoba I fall in love with the Arab houses all over again. They seem to have all that can possibly be required for civilized anti-social existence, thick walls, wide stairways, airy rooms and great doors that are truly shut when they are shut. How pleasant to be safe behind such doors with picked companions, in a cool rather dark room arranged in the uncosy unfussy Andalusian way, the scent of rose and geranium in the blazing sun outside and the sound of falling water!

Thus we never saw Góngora's house but went off to drink Montilla wine instead. If it is pleasant to have an aim it is also, in Andalusia, unwise to pursue it with fanaticism. And it might be said that Cordoba is Góngora's house and Cordoba is his poetry. The sun was going down, and across the river the flocks and herds were coming down to drink. Lines of mules in red trappings trotted nose to tail with piles of green clover, or baskets of tools, or men, on their backs. Outside

San Nicolas de la Villa stood the familiar sinister glass cage and black-plumed horses, horses and plumes both covered in dust, while through the open door came glimpses of black velvet drapery, candlelight flickering over gold and silver ornament and priests, intoning in their harsh nasal voices. Reverently placed in the main square by the Spanish Army five hundred years after his birth, the *Gran Capitán* tranquilly bestrode his charger amid the hurly-burly there. At the half-hour and the hour a guitar strummed a few bars of flamenco through a loudspeaker, and then in tantalizing fashion fell quiet. The sky turned a soft apricot, then green and finally indigo and the stars came out one by one.

In Spain, perhaps everywhere else but particularly in Spain, no sooner are positive general statements made than they begin to seem untrue. That two and two make four is all that can be asserted with total confidence. Thus, having said Cordoba does not change, I begin to see all manner of objections or exceptions. The superficial changes going on all over the country at present are of course found here as well, if rather more hesitantly, as may be expected in so conservative a region. The hotels are bringing themselves into line with European thought by charging European prices, while showing a sound Andalusian independence by maintaining the standards of yore. Women, even unaccompanied, are seen in the cafés more frequently. Beggars no longer mob you, people wait quietly in queues for their buses, even though the queue flies apart when the bus appears, and, unless I'm a Dutchman, the main water-supply has some abominable medication in it.

One real change that has come about in recent years, however, is the disappearance as such of the cenobite monks or hermits of Cordoba. Their tradition dates from the time of Bishop Osio the Good in the third century, surviving wars, Moorish and Arab occupation and the Council of Trent,

spanning sixteen hundred years of troubled history only to be
swept into the Carmelite Order in 1957. They were rude
rough people, living scattered over the mountain above the
city in solitude and privation and meeting only for Mass and
in Communion.

To reach them there is a drive of seven kilometres from the
Plaza José Antonio through the garden suburb of El Brillante
north of the city and up a road winding about the hillside of the
Sierra Morena, with herds of ginger pigs with floppy ears
rooting for acorns among the scrub. There is a *mirador* halfway
up with a superb view over Cordoba and the plain beyond, as
well as the velvety green flank of the mountain itself. And here
again there is change. Only quite a short time ago we should
have seen from this point roughly what the hermits saw
throughout the Middle Ages: now the eye is afflicted by
numerous ugly great buildings, such as the Polytechnic to the
west and the Jesuit seminary immediately below.

Once past the *mirador* the car turns away up a rough stony
track, which ends abruptly at the doors of the hermitage itself.
The last time but one I visited it we were received and taken
round by a smiling monk with the rosy transparent complexion
of people who eat hardly at all and live in the open air, who
talked freely and gaily without stopping. This time a sallow,
disagreeable individual in a smudged brown habit thrust a
greasy sheet of typed information into my hand and waved
me speechlessly on to the interior. He looked far more like a
garage hand than a holy contemplative and, in fact, was soon
engaged in a bawling match with the driver.

The visitor is first welcomed and made to feel at home by a
skull which peeps from a cavity in a stone pillar above this
little verse:

> *Como te ves, yo me ví,*
> *Como me ves, te veras,*
> *Todo para en esto, aquí;*
> *Piensalo, y no pecarás.*

(As you see yourself, I saw myself, as you see me you will
see yourself, All ends in this, here; Think of it and you will
not sin.)

Next comes the hermitage of St Mary Magdalene, unused
to-day and shown as a pattern of all the thirteen others which
one can see, little white cabins nestling among the shrubs,
flowers and sweet herbs of the mountain. It has two tiny
rooms with furnishings of the plainest: a wooden bed with a
straw mat to sleep on and a rough sheepskin for a covering, a
candil or primitive oil dip as the only light, one or two coarse
pots, a frying-pan over the fire, and a wooden shepherd's
crook. There were besides a crucifix and a rosary, a skull of
course, a scourge of knotted ropes and a book of devotions
put together by one of the Bishops of Mondoñedo in Galicia.
A verse on the wall said that to mortify the flesh was good but
to subdue the will, or pride, was better.

I went on to the hermits' cemetery which was of the white
plaster chest-of-drawers type found in Spanish villages and
washed white. One black vacant hole always yawns wide for
the next to come, and there is a pit of bones behind. Here
again there are two skulls, snug in their little caves, eyeing
the stranger with their characteristic look of blank amusement.

There is also a tiny church that clearly must be a source of
lamentable pride to the hermits, for they have collected
together in it every hideous object that can ever have been
donated to them. To the left of the porch as you enter is a
horrific painting of *El Alma en Pecado* (Soul in Sin) and to the
right one of a grinning bucolic red-nosed wench which is *El
Alma en Gracia* (Soul in state of Grace): it is a real puzzle to
know which invites us the less. There are chandeliers, vases,
candlesticks, good pictures, bad pictures, terrible pictures,
statues and the dear Lord only knows what, till the effect is
often like the *salon* of some particularly awful *pension*. It is

curious to think that men who feast their eyes on the mountain and the plain all day long can endure the sight of this.

Now, following the trend of the day, they are all *cerrados* or enclosed and each must remain within his whitewashed hive except when called by the church bell. The dogged anchorites held out through all those hundreds of years only to lose themselves in the featureless wastes of the twentieth century. Such cases do exist elsewhere in Spain, but this is one of them to be most regretted. We cannot help thinking of what Charles V said in 1526 to the Canons of Cordoba Mosque when he viewed the *capilla mayor* that Hernán Ruiz had obtruded on it: "Had I known what you desired to do, you would not have done it, for what you are doing here can be found everywhere and what you possessed previously exists nowhere."

❧ 7 ❧

THINGS THAT LOOK DIFFICULT ELSEWHERE, IN SPAIN
will often be mysteriously simple. Others that elsewhere are
simplicity itself, in Spain are fraught with inexplicable compli-
cation.

As a notable example of this, we may cite Spanish railways
and all to do with them. A terrible beauty hovers over the
entire field of their being and doing. Years ago I inquired the
purpose of an enormous building, or set of buildings, near
Malaga and was told it was for the orphans of railroad workers.
Even with the assumption that it was the only one of its kind,
it somehow left the impression that mortality in this social
group was strangely high. Later on I put the same question
in respect of more huge buildings, this time outside Avila,
and got the same reply. And I have received it since, in various
other places, whose names for the moment escape me. Railway
orphans appear to occupy in Spanish vital statistics a place
similar to that of lunatics in the Irish.

A time of waiting in a Spanish station will provide almost
endless food for thought, appropriately enough, as the waiting
all too often will seem endless as well. After hours of torpor,
Spanish trains will suddenly utter harrowing cries or make
furious little rushes to and fro that, to the uninstructed, seem
quite irrelevant and uncalled-for. A third-class-only Local
of faded purplish brown wood, or that most terrible form of
transport, the *Mixto*, a combination of Passenger and Goods
that is to the ordinary Slow (here called *rápido*) what the Slow
is to the Express: some lower form of ferroviarian life, I say,

that has stood motionless and packed to the brim for hours in the blistering sun will all at once, without a word to or from a soul, slip quietly away, as a crocodile will suddenly slip off the bank and into the river. Or when at last the TAF is on the point of arriving, at a platform black with stoical Spaniards and peevish tourists, a Goods drawn up in a siding will for no apparent reason other than its own caprice gatecrash the party, shunting importantly up, muttering and hissing, its individual carriages cannoning into each other like clumsy folk-dancers, before rumbling away again whence it came.

No doubt there is good reason for their behaviour, if one but knew it. The little train that puffs and groans its way from Malaga up to Coin has a bloodcurdling shriek that alarms people greatly when they hear it for the first time. But the purpose of those banshee howls is merely to scare elephants off the line ahead. The engine was constructed by a Belgian firm, who intended it for the Congo. Once you know these things, they appear natural and sound and, indeed, obvious.

Whatever the extent of their knowledge, this form of Spanish travel is still not recommended to any but those of a ruminant cast of mind. Apart from all else, it is full of unexpected little *guet-apens*. People accustomed at home to buy a ticket and jump on any train they like can hardly be expected to guess that here, as far as the main lines go, they must reserve one particular seat on one particular train, and that no other will do.

This was well rubbed into me on the Barcelona-Saragossa express one day. The concierge of the hotel in Barcelona had sent a *mozo* to buy the ticket and he, with his mind running on his personal affairs, came back with the wrong one. Barcelona likes to think itself above the rest of Spain in these matters so that perhaps the *mozo* was not a true Catalan; but he bought a ticket for the *rápido* that left in the middle of the night instead of the morning express.

The guard came through the compartments at the last

moment to see that all was in order – the limits to Spanish anarchy are a subject of immense fascination – and told me to get off. I ought, he said, to have travelled the night before. Friends were going to meet me at a fixed time outside the Old Cathedral in Saragossa and we had agreed on no alternative in case of failure, a precarious arrangement anywhere and in Spain stark lunacy. I begged for *clemencia*. Outside on the platform a bell was tolling, no need to send to know for whom as the locomotive by now was grunting impatiently and the guard shouted that I alone was holding things up. He seized my suitcase and trotted away with it, turning hopefully to see if I were following, as a dog trots away with a glove to encourage you to take him out, and exploding with fury when he saw me there immobile.

But in Spain more often than not the accident or error that sets us fuming and fretting will lead to an experience as delightful as instructive. One by one the three men in the compartment now took the matter up, crying that it was a disgrace to the country and that the foreigner should be left in peace. The guard rushed away and came back with a kind of *Vaterfigur* in a resplendent uniform, and furious altercation broke out between the five. It was not, however, the troubles of any foreigner that enraged the passengers but the idea of authority itself, incarnate in the two officials.

The bell tolled on and I could picture my friends waiting sadly outside the cathedral hour after hour.

The guard seized the case again and trotted out, and one of the passengers bounded after him and snatched it away. The *Vaterfigur* disappeared, as if loth to put his powers to any further test. A shindy broke out and mounted to a pitch where the clangour of a mere bell was all swallowed up and it looked as if violence would follow. I harkened spellbound to the mighty voices until, glancing idly out of the window, I saw a thing that filled my heart with peace and love. The train had left the station and was running smoothly through the smoky

74

outskirts of Barcelona to the pleasant country beyond. No Spaniard, official or not, would ever be barbarous enough to strand a person now. The issue was no longer a live one and yet the four of them continued to hurl arguments at each other with unflagging zest until, quite suddenly and for no apparent reason, it all died down and the guard went away. Now and then he put in his head at the door to smile at me, and when the man who in fact was entitled to my place got in at Reus he was hurried off to the other end of the train.

It then became clear that all the time the guard too had been but shadow-boxing, that he too was stoutly opposed to authority even while clad in its trappings and that he regarded his own defeat as a triumph for justice and common sense.

These two desirable things prevail far more often in Spain than is commonly believed; but they do not always and are very likely not to where money is involved, money being one of the half-dozen or so things that Spaniards can take seriously. Thus it is important to be familiar with another strange ferroviarian rule, namely, that if you jump on to a train without a ticket you will have to pay double fare when the inspector comes round.

All these are but technicalities, fringe activities. More fundamental is the problem of how to get on a train at all without bribing about as many people as if you intended to start a railway line of your own. The TAF from Malaga to Cordoba had been three-quarters empty and it therefore seemed a simple matter to buy a place on it up to Madrid. The *concierge* said it would be very difficult indeed. He said it would in fact be impossible, except that fortunately the hotel possessed a *mozo* who enjoyed the confidence of a *mozo* in the station, and this second *mozo* was on a footing of reciprocated esteem with higher station authority. I informed the *concierge* that the station-master was a cousin of my godfather and hurried down to draw the coverts.

A man in ragged blue *mozo*'s uniform who had been fast

asleep on a bench in the sun opened one eye at my approach, as if alerted by some mysterious agency to a chance not to be thrown away. The object of overwhelming interest about this man was his nose, which resembled an enormous ripe strawberry: it was a nose into which years of patient effort must have gone, a nose in a million. He observed that it was lucky I had run into him, for he was the one man in the station who could *arreglar* my affair. I asked him what was to prevent me going myself to the TAF *taquilla* when it opened and buying a ticket. He responded readily that nothing did, but it would be imprudent, for only a few tickets were left to-day and I was unknown, whereas his own *relaciones* with the ticket vendor were *buenísimas*. I asked what he expected for the service and he replied with a fruity chuckle he would leave this to me, but the more I gave him, the better.

What I did may be considered wrong by many, perhaps indeed by all except the *mozo*. It will be said that such people ought not to be encouraged and that such make life harder for the foreign resident, as distinct from the mere bird of passage: but replies are possible to all that. Foreigners in Spain should humbly recognize that their principal charm is their money, and their only virtue, a readiness to part with it. The cry we so often hear, "A Spaniard would have given half," is all very well, but we are not Spaniards. If we were, we should probably be trying to feed four or five children on £12 a month. And I always feel inclined to laugh when Anglo-Saxons reproach me with helping to make life harder for them "out here" because, except in a very few cases, I would view with composure the prospect of its being made impossible. Finally, it was a treat and a privilege to contribute a mite towards the upkeep of that magnificent nose: the desire to be in even a modest way associated with notable enterprises is a very human and respectable one.

Accordingly, the *mozo* was entrusted with the little affair and he carried it through to perfection, as well he might, for it was simplicity itself. He received his unexpectedly ample tip with the *sangre fría* of long habit, although the great nose seemed for an instant to burn a brighter red, and placed me in the charge of another official who, he said, would help me on to the train and escort me to a seat. This, for some reason, it was beyond his own power to do. Again, could this not be done without help? Of course, the Señora could do as she liked, but it was more fitting to let others do it for her so as to spare herself the annoyance of struggles and litigation.

By now the news that a mug of no mean order was at large in the area had flashed from one platform to the next and columns of ragged gipsy boys with water, bananas, chewing-gum, pea-nuts and caramels for sale were converging implacably on me. Altogether it was a relief to see the pale blunt nose of the TAF sliding round the corner. The two coaches comprising it were barely half full but the official leaped upon it at once, cleaving a way through phantom crowds and fending off invisible assailants with great determination, and threw my luggage on to a seat. He collected his own *propina* and smilingly bowed himself away. Through the window I saw my friend, *el de la nariz*, composing himself to sleep on the bench again. The TAF gave its heartrending cry and rattled off into the unknown.

The way to get the best and deepest pleasure from travel in Spain is to go very casually and not too hopefully, to be ready for a switch of plan at any moment and to accept with calm whatever may befall. By no means everything that goes awry is a disaster. It was, for example, by a happy fluke that I learned how captivating Burgos can be in the depths of winter. I was going from Irun to Madrid on the TALGO, that most delightful of conveyances, so comfortable, so fast, so *moderno*, humping and twisting like a silver caterpillar so easily through the mountain bends, slowing down so kindly as it runs by the huge pale mass of the Escorial: it may well be something to do with the line at that point which causes it to slow but equally it may be in order that we can all have a good look at the Escorial and tell our friends that we have seen it. An excellent meal had been brought to the passengers in their comfortable chairs and everyone was happy and relaxed and wreathed in cigar smoke. It was hard to believe our ears in Burgos station when all at once we were peppered with orders to leave our places and come out. Everything else in the world might break down but not the TALGO: one would as soon expect the *Queen Elizabeth* to founder in mid-ocean. Officials raced up and down the platform bawling at us in the loud angry voices Spaniards use when they feel sorry and ashamed about something they cannot help. We all stumbled shivering into the icy air and ran to the telegraph office or plagued the officials with inquiries. All they could promise was just sometime, midnight perhaps, Madrid would send out a *rápido*. Why torment oneself? I went in search of a good hotel, found it in the Condestable, heated to a glorious tropical warmth, and moved in.

It was only later as I wandered through the town that it became clear how considerate the TALGO had been. Burgos the rugged wore a new and enchanting face in the sharp Castilian frost that powdered trees, shrubs, flowers and statues, sparkling without melting in the sun. The river rushed through the middle of the city in its full winter strength, foaming and tumbling about the rocks and boulders in its bed. The dry river beds of summer with their caking mud and bleached rocks, their sparse puddles reflecting the sky, are so familiar a part of the Spanish landscape that a torrent of pure mountain water comes as a wonderfully enlivening and dramatic surprise. Everything else had a severe clean northern look as well: the pavements rang like iron underfoot: the trees lining the streets were pollarded to weird and fanciful shapes.

Suddenly round a corner rose up the twin towers of the cathedral, most wonderful of Gothic cathedrals, a huge pile of stone so lightly and delicately put together that it seems about to float away. It had never looked more exquisite than now with the towers leaping against a sky the soft apricot colour of winter evenings in Castile, the silvery grey of the façade mellowing into a gentle opal haze. The doors should have opened at three o'clock but at a quarter to five were still shut. A policeman said that a new bishop was to be consecrated on the following day and doubtless they were making all preparations within. I waited for a long time, wandering through the cloisters and round the *crucero*, returning in the end always to those magical spires which now seemed to have drawn in all the colour that had left the sky and to be glowing with it as flowers glow at dusk. Still the doors were shut and on the policeman's advice I gave it up and went for a stroll round the town. It was after six and the evening *paseo* was just beginning. Droves of young girls were promenading bareheaded and in light shoes, frozen to the marrow, watched admiringly by the young men and satirically by the vendors of roasted chestnuts beside their charcoal *braseros*. The horses' hooves beat sparks out of the road and the frosty cobbles and pavings scintillated in the lamplight: the boughs of the shrubs and trees in the formal gardens were furry with rime. Burgos that evening looked like a city in fairyland, and I owed it all to the TALGO.

The next day was freezing and sunless with a mist hanging over the river and the distant hills. It was the eve of Epiphany and on the steps of the cathedral a number of workmen were setting up a crib for the Three Kings with wood and green branches and straw. On and on they laboured, never speaking or looking round, grave and preoccupied as only Spanish workmen would be with such a task. Inside the cathedral the consecration was about to begin. Someone had left a pile of vestments on the High Altar and the sacristans were unrolling a long threadbare red carpet down the body of the building for the new bishop to walk on. Presently he appeared, with a number of priests round him, who sat down comfortably while he was robed for Mass. Two old women in black shawls, an old man with a gleaming bald head and myself composed the entire congregation, but it seemed to be a private affair anyhow. In the middle of the Mass the bishop broke off and muttered an address to the clergy who were sitting round on chairs in a horseshoe, the whole affair being attractively casual and unpompous and the scene charming under the great gold *retablo* with the little Madonna and Child illumined in the centre. The whole edifice meanwhile resounded, like every cathedral in Spain to-day, to the mighty hammer-blows of workmen.

The people of Burgos suit their cathedral in their happy combination of dignity and grace. They seem wholly northern in temperament in a way that the Madrileños do not and the men have a strong typical cast of feature. In the *retablo* of the high altar at Miraflores Carthusian monastery, Our Lord and His apostles look very *burgalés*, and not of the peasant or fisherman class either but the solid professional kind that belongs to clubs. There is some interesting and homely detail in this *retablo*, by the way: both Our Lord and Saint James the Elder appear to have divergent squints and on the table is a dish of sucking-pig with a mustard pot beside it, while a miniature Magdalene crawls on the floor like a baby and strokes her Redeemer's feet. Sucking-pig at the Last Supper is an item supported, as far as I know, neither by authority nor tradition and we can only think the mediaeval artist was so fond of it himself as to seize every chance of portraying it. The Castilian passion for those insipid and glutinous blobs of jelly must go a long way back.

These are good people to deal with, being not only honest themselves but taking honesty for granted in others. If you want something in a shop without having enough money on you they will beg you to take the thing and pay another time. The charming point of the transaction is that when you bring the money in they look neither pleased nor surprised: the emotions of a Neapolitan similarly placed may be imagined. And their humour has the Castilian bite to it, the sardonic rasp that goes with their grim and often terrible land. The quip a waiter made when I queried a luxury tax of ten per cent. on my bill after lunch was an instance. In general I am all for the luxury tax, for if we are able to enjoy and indulge ourselves in so poor a country by all means let us pay for it. Besides, Spaniards are fanatically opposed to any form of taxation whatever and the State must get its revenue from somewhere. I could not see, however, in what way an omelette and salad, a glass of wine and a cup of coffee constituted *lujo*, a word suggestive of champagne, strawberries in winter and chorus girls baked in pies. The waiter made short work of it. "Haven't you eaten?" he asked. "Isn't that lujo?"

At this moment they were all wholeheartedly preparing for the Feast of the Epiphany, which as far as sheer revelry goes is a bigger one in all Spain than Christmas itself. Music, religious and secular, roared from loudspeakers all over the city, pleasure and noise being to the Latin mind synonymous. The workmen had completed the crib and shrouded it in sacking and a little crowd of people of all ages and conditions were standing round it and eagerly trying to peer in. It was a bad day for business of any kind because nobody could bear to sit still. Even the little page at the Condestable who was devoured by ambition and saved up all his tips for a passage to America left bells to ring and doors to open themselves while he stood, shivering, on the front steps in case something noteworthy went by. As the day passed the streets grew more and more crowded and snow began to fall, which seemed to amuse everybody. Two vast yellow oxen drawing a cart up the main street paced on, despite the appeals of the drover, with such imperturbable unhurrying calm that the whole ensemble was trimmed with snow.

In the evening, naturally, there was a procession. The snow in the roadways had been trodden hard and smooth and brilliant like the icing on a cake and the mounts of the standard bearers slithered wildly from side to side. A crowd of little boys dressed as crusaders followed, saucing the onlookers as they came, in marked contrast to the indescribable solemnity of their elders. Next came mounted Hussars with spiked helmets and a military jingling of spur and bridle, then more cheeky little boys, now in Moorish costume, and finally the Three Kings themselves. Frenzied applause broke out for Gaspar the Negro, as he rolled his eyes in his sooty face and adjusted his shaky crown. The rear was brought up by a multitude on horseback, also skating wildly about the road until the scene began to resemble a pantomime on ice. Confusion was added by youths walking alongside and waving huge lighted torches over their heads to the alarm and indignation of horse and mule. Every other moment diabolical Spanish rockets leaped upwards writhing and whistling into the sky although, *Deo gratias*, many of them failed to explode. Lost in contemplation I did not notice until the procession had gone by that I was slowly turning to ice. The dense crowds that were following the Three Kings to the bitter end filled me with a new admiration for the Spanish people: burning heat, pouring rain, arctic cold, nothing daunts them in the pursuit of pleasure. And this was but a rehearsal for the following day, a pale sketch of what was to come; and out again all the good people would come and stand by the hour in the cruel frost.

From away up the hillside beyond the old wall Burgos had the fairyland look again that night. The cathedral illumined was a miracle of delicacy and grace. The dark mass of the town stood out against the white enveloping uplands and the sound of bells and faint voices came drifting up from it. There was a tawny fringe to the clouds about the moon, and a deep silence over the land, the silence that comes from far away and atones for the roar of cities.

It is said that Spaniards do not understand the machine and it is also said that they understand it but are not prepared to meet it halfway. Their view, some have thought, is that machines should go of their own accord and that service and maintenance are simply frills. Without hazarding any assertion I wonder if there is not a touch of mysticism in their attitude, a sense that the world is one great roulette-board and all planning and pre-arranging is doomed to failure. Will she make it? will she? the driver of a crowded bus may be pondering as she grinds up an all but perpendicular road. A duller, more earthbound man would have cleaned the plugs, mended the leak in the radiator and adjusted the brakes before ever he started out. Very likely our driver sees no connection between fuss of that kind and the vehicle's performance, which he sees as a matter for God. He and his passengers will arrive in safety *si Dios quiere* and if not, then not.

It is also alleged by some that Spaniards do not care if they live or die, and Spain is indeed a land of wild and preposterous death. A workman will proudly show off a stick of explosive to friends clustered round it puffing away at their cigarettes until heads, arms and legs fly through the air in every direction. A man asks a friend to give him an injection of his own prescription and on his own diagnosis and dies within the hour. Another man electrocutes himself on the live cable running through his field, knowing quite well that it is there. As for maimings and disfigurements, there is no end to it: as Mr Gerald Brenan has said, Spaniards shed their arms and legs like crabs. Here again the usual explanations strike me as erroneous or incomplete. I believe Spaniards care too deeply for life to be cautious with it and that they are too passionately alive not to be excited and attracted by death; and this is perhaps why they value physical courage above any other.

Such were the thoughts that flitted through my mind as I sat fuming in the Burgos-Madrid coach on that Feast of the Epiphany. My sunny thoughts on the function of accident in travel had vanished for, extravagant as it may seem, this coach had broken down as well. It chose for the purpose a remote icy road in the Sierra Guadarrama, plentifully supplied with arctic winds and looking on to a panorama of Siberian desolation. Here and there at the side of the road twisting away down behind us were the whitening bones of jettisoned vehicles, and heaven only knew what grisly matters within them. For us there seemed but the choice of freezing to death in the open air or suffocating and possibly burning alive within. Directly the great coffin-like lid of the engine was opened a little fountain of petrol began to play and all the men on board rushed forward to examine it, puffing at their cigars as they went. Each man began to shout advice, believing that he and he alone should direct the operation. The driver sat with folded arms like a man in a dream: there was something terrible in that quiet despair. The coach coming back from Madrid now drew up alongside and all aboard laughed heartily as our predicament became known. Two fainthearts among us got out and transferred with their innumerable bundles to the already crammed Burgos coach, whose driver and conductor hastened over to pool their intellectual resources with ours. The strange conductor said there was a leak of petrol and our driver seemed to come alive. He leaped as if he had been stung and shouted something, and then lapsed into his unnerving gloom once more. All at once the coach began to bowl smoothly backwards and the men hurled themselves at the brakes while the women screamed. Our conductor took up an old wooden box and, as the key could not be found, skilfully picked the lock. Inside was an assortment of articles intended, no doubt, for just such an emergency as the present, screws, tins, bits of old rubber tubing, half a windscreen wiper and an assortment of rags, including a knitted stocking. The people in the other coach were still laughing. Our conductor chose out the better pieces of rubber tubing, holding them up against the fluffy grey sky to test for holes. One of them seemed to appeal to him more than the rest, for he gave it a loving little pat before inserting it somewhere deep in the monster's entrails. Next he firmly bound the stocking above the leak. *Vamos!*

84

The driver shrugged and gingerly started the engine up and the monster crept a few paces forward, moaning and hissing as it went. Shouts of applause came from the other coach, whose occupants had apparently been content to sit and contemplate us for ever, and their driver and conductor hastily rejoined them, arguing vivaciously all the time. Again we set off, the women crossing themselves several times over as if to be sure they'd made a job of it and the men speculating on the chances of reaching Madrid that night, or at all. The driver accelerated, listening to the engine's cries with all the anguish of a mother for her suffering child. Soon we were racing along at full speed, swinging round corners and hogging the road in completely normal fashion, but with a strong smell of petrol. Will she make it? will she? Yesterday the TALGO, to-day the coach. Next week I must take the aeroplane to Malaga. . . . By this time we had reached the pass and on the other side was a dense mountain mist. Now we had to creep forward inch by inch with a terrifying sense of walking a tight-rope. We shall be hours and hours late in Madrid but we shall get there all right, in perfect safety: *si Dios quiere*. Spain would bring out the mystic in anyone.

❧ *8* ❧

IF BELIEF THAT SPIRITUAL ASSUMPTIONS LIE BEHIND the material ups and downs of Spanish life should falter a corrective is to drive out of Madrid to the Valle de los Caidos, on the way to the Escorial. There these same people who cannot or will not keep an engine in repair or persuade a tap to run have hewn a mighty basilica out of living rock. The setting is one of rare grandeur. From far away a gigantic cross can be seen leaping skywards from its rough pedestal of pink and yellow rock, a spectacular and flamboyant memorial that appears complete in itself. The natural twisted rock studded with dog-rose and cistus and broom runs round three sides of it and in front is a formal *encinta* with steps up to the portals of the great man-made cave. Above the entrance is a *pietas* and on either side within an angel of death, for inside the church are the remains of some of the fallen in the Civil War: these remains were taken from the dead of both sides, which seems a little mad, but the whole thing is mad, a piece of stupendous, endearing, Spanish *locura*. The mints of money could not have been better spent. It may be that the images and furnishings and iron grilles are crude and unappealing but this is usual in religious art to-day; at least, the proportions are fine and there is an outstanding crucifix on the High Altar. From the white Benedictine monastery in the rear with the rows of tiny dark windows and lines of silvery poplar comes relayed the placid growl of monks chanting the Hours, to soothe a little the uneasiness that the dedication might arouse with the reminder of things that outlast the quarrels and blunders of men. And

86

genius has gone into the choice of the Risco de la Nava as the building site too, for the view is finer than all, a great sweep over a wild valley with umbrella pines and craggy boulders to the mountains far off, the trees and shrubs bowed under the weight of snow in winter, in summer gay with butterflies and flowers.

There are booklets on sale to say how many workers laboured for how many years on the job, figures that summon up a vision of toiling sweating gasping crowds such as dragged up the stones of the Pyramids. The Spanish love of the grandiose and the extravagant here got the better of the torpor that results from the Spanish sense of ultimate futility. As with many of the warring Spanish qualities the two are balanced so well that a perpetual seesaw goes on, with an area of calm Spanish compromise lying between: a compromise which consists of avoiding effort because it must end in failure and at the same time behaving as if the effort had already and successfully been made.

I remember a baker in Andalusia who availed himself of this felicitous combination to the full. He believed that he was no ordinary baker but an artist as well: he was too sure of himself to make much of it but he felt the plenitude of artistry in all his daily life. Unable to bear the thought of his masterpieces being wrongly attributed he marked every loaf with his initials before it went into the oven. When his boy left it at the door you knew that it was the genuine article, *bajo su firma*, the flourish of it unaffected by even the hardest baking.

The satisfying thing, and the one relevant to our discussion, was that the bread was terrible. The Andalusian loaf is a dough-pat of remarkable density at the best of times. Under-baked it is soggy, and baked too long its crust grows like the bark of a tree. Our baker merrily alternated between the two techniques. Veins of flour ran through the loaves and great caverns yawned at their hearts, for mixing and kneading followed a dance of their own as well.

No one said anything to him. No one said much to anyone else although sometimes of an evening the village elders, seated on the benches round the fountain, would refer in tones of piercing sadness to bread they had eaten in their youth. The baker was protected by the magic of those initials: clothed in an idea he warded reality off and the suffering *pueblo* esteemed him for it and respected the fantasy. The Spanish word *ilusión* has the same meaning as the English *illusion* in the dictionary, but echoes differently in the mind. To us, illusion is a weakness to recognize and overcome: to a Spaniard his *ilusión* gives the world its glow and life its fragrance. Only a barbarian would rob a man of it.

Men like this baker, living in the favourable weather of their own minds, are to be found in every corner of the land. Whatever the differences that exist, and so often are exaggerated, between Andalusian and Galician, Basque and Catalan, this peculiarity is fairly general. Indeed, the place where I came on it once in a form so extreme as to verge on the macabre was hardheaded, come-no-nonsense old Barcelona. In a dreary little night-club, a kind of hole in the wall, I spent an evening that might have come out of a story by Thomas Mann. I have forgotten the club's name and the street it was in, but the way to it led through the Barrio Chino, which must be one of the last red-light districts in Europe.

It was raw and foggy, as it often is in Barcelona, and the horns of the ships in harbour blew steadily and mournfully as if calling on mankind to repent. Tipsy foreign sailors stumbled along the narrow ill-lighted streets and ogled the women clustering in doorways. Shouts and bursts of raucous song came from the bars, and the shop-windows were crammed with an assortment of prophylactics and remedies for dire complaints. Men came trickling out of the squalid houses with an expression of face that recalled a line of Ovid, and it was electrifying to see, among it all, a signboard on a first-floor balcony which read: *Colegio para señoritas*.

To get to the club we had to go through a provision store, a homely place with strings of sausages, tins of tomato paste, piles of fat bacon and barrels of chick peas. An old man was counting the money in the till and did not look up. We went down some steps to a smoky little dive containing a dozen or so tables, a rickety stage about eight feet across and a piano at the back of it. The walls were dark and the room was decorated with tawdry ropes of bunting, artificial flowers, signed photographs and cheap china vases like the junk in a seaside lodging house.

The Spaniard with me had hinted at new and startling experience and he sat there now sipping cognac and looking thoroughly complacent. There were few other people in the dive and by their appearance those few might have been resting from their endeavours in the Barrio Chino. A young man with a sulky face jumped on the stage and struck up a *paso doble* on the tinny piano. Then the star of the evening made his entry. Dressed in a white flannel suit and a straw boater like a musical comedy hero of the twenties he came, shaking a tambourine over his head and uttering gay excited little cries. The audience paid no attention at all and yet he bowed and smiled and kissed his hand as he went as if acknowledging the tumultuous applause of a multitude. He climbed slowly and painfully on to the stage, putting a hand to his back, and then swept the boater from his head with a gesture that again seemed to be a response to frenzied acclamation.

He was a wrinkled old man of seventy-odd with dull eyes and false teeth. First he sang a number of romantic songs in French, winking and leering as he went and treating us to a flow of patter between each one. He was, he said, a *chansonnier* in the good old tradition just as Maurice Chevalier was, and by the way he executed *Paris! Paris!* he was clearly of the opinion that Chevalier could teach him nothing. Then he would dance a little, flinging his creaky old limbs about with an occasional rictus of pain. He had brought with him an armful of astounding

89

props, wigs, a matador's *traje de luces*, an evening jacket heavily fringed to look like a shawl, a red reefer coat such as a young masher might wear; and into these he would change in full view of the audience, smiling his old man's nutcracker smile as he did so. His numerous acts were sandwiched by horrifying performances from old women. An elderly dwarf sang, or rather screamed, *O Sole Mio* in a voice that resembled a factory hooter. So excruciating were her notes that even her hardened public would sometimes have to gasp or cry. After her an older woman still, dressed in a spangled skirt and *mantilla*, her face heavily rouged, howled *Valencia* as she skipped about the stage and tossed carnations into the smoky air. She had but a few teeth left and her face had seemingly been knocked or squashed out of alignment but she screeched away like a stimulated cockatoo, throwing glances full of love towards my young escort. There followed a giantess, her enormous lolling bosom and hips squeezed into the tightest of sweaters and skirts and her hair dyed a ferocious yellow: with the assured strength of a carthorse she roared away of love and passion and her suffering heart until one thought of the fattest whore with the true, beautiful memories in Hemingway's *Light of the World*.

All their songs were like that, all treated of love and youth and fidelity, roses, jasmine and moonlight, not in a spirit of nostalgia or recollection but as if the singers still participated. The flesh crept to see them grimace and shut their eyes and lay their wrinkled hands on their breasts as their voices precariously wobbled on. And they all received the room's perfunctory, ironic applause in the same way. Like great and beloved singers who are rejoiced and overwhelmed by the enthusiasm of thousands, they made deprecating little gestures, they bowed low in feigned humility, they blew kisses to their sniggering fans, with a sweep of the arm they included the pianist in their triumph. He, poor youth, never looked round and clearly would do naught beyond what he was paid for.

It was horrible, it was Grand Guignol, but it was not sad because these people were safe in their *ilusión*. They were not poor crocks desperately trying to make a few last pesetas before vanishing into whatever asylum or lazar-house awaited their lonely age. They supposed their talent was such that the passing of time could never affect it, that despite the years they could still create an impression of radiance and youth. The chamber of horrors in which they operated was a centre of art and culture and gaiety. They read with absolute gravity the occasional mock-respectful allusions to them in the newspapers. Each, it was said, kept a supply of autographed portraits to bestow on admirers. And ever in their ears there echoed the ghostly clapping of thousands of phantom hands.

We had looked in for an hour at ten o'clock and it was nearly two when at last we got up to go. I had been sitting in a kind of trance. The old man rushed across the room and demanded "Was I good to-night?" There was no interrogation in his voice and he did not listen to the reply. With an indescribable lordliness of manner he told us we were always welcome in his cabaret. We left him grinning in senile gratification and went past the dangling sausages and the chick peas and pickled anchovies out to the street. The quarter was animated still, there were lights in the cafés and bars and little yellow taxicabs crawled up and down like beetles searching for prey. The respectable parts of the great city were hushed and dark as the dwellers there recouped their powers in order to rise again next day and earn Spain's living for her.

It was long before I fell asleep, for the extraordinary things we had seen kept running through my mind. My companion had not been boasting when he undertook to show something that could hardly be found anywhere else. But things peculiar to Spain, and they are many, will none the less often relate themselves in the weirdest way to human life in general. I felt uneasily that what we had been watching in the grisly little night-club was but an aspect of ourselves, and my disquiet persisted into sleep, resulting in dreams that strangely mingled the familiar and the monstrous.

I was roused by a dreadful screaming, such as might be expected of a fiend in hell. Another joined in and then another, all together in a wild tormented limitless howling as if the whole company of the damned were chorusing in despair. Only once in my life before had I heard anything like it, and that was the howling monkey of the Amazon forest. The shrieking rose and fell, rose and fell, drew nearer, a horrible menacing sound that seemed to me in my drowsy state to be somehow connected with the events of the evening. Yet I harkened to it enthralled, carried away by the sheer demoniac frenzy of those terrible voices. Now they passed below the window and I ran eagerly for a sight of the devils, if such they were, but it was only fire-engines, the splendid, passionate, crazy fire-engines of Barcelona. How different their cry from the prosaic sirens of England or the querulous pam-pom pam-pom of France! All through my stay there they woke me nearly every night, and I loved them for it, I loved and reverenced their very madness. I never found anyone else to share this taste, however, and somebody thought it must be Arab.

It is not only in material undertakings that a continual oscillation between fierce energy and complete apathy appears to go on. "Love God as He is and not as you imagine Him to be," was the dry counsel of a Spanish theologian who knew the deforming violence of which his compatriots' imagination is capable. Yet this same religious imagination is often so lazy as to need the monstrous or the absurd to get it working at all. To enter into the agony of the Cross it requires the horrifying visual representation of a tortured body with ghastly face and gaping streaming wounds: the majesty of the Virgin will have to be conveyed to it by a childish robing and adorning and bejewelling: skulls and bones will be strewn about the floor to encourage it to a sense of mortality. The renowned Spanish realism is nothing but a kind of cerebral flagellation. A typical if extreme case was the *pudridero* in the Escorial where, to emphasize that kings and queens share equally in the vileness of the flesh and its ultimate humiliation, the royal corpses were left to rot and stink awhile before their interment. Even the greatest Spanish minds appear subject to bouts of lethargy, when the hollowness within seems like the extension of a universal void, and the sufferer feels like one of those inflated hogskins ballooning in the wind under the cruel suns of Estremadura. The "aridity" of soul which tormented Teresa de Jesús and which she looked on as the deliberate withdrawal by God of His presence may have been no more than the great swing of the pendulum from ecstasy to exhaustion. In that very Spanish book, *Del Sentimiento Trágico de la Vida*, Unamuno ascribes the lack of a wish for immortality in certain individuals as the ultimate form of sloth: a most delightful idea and one that would hardly occur to anyone but a Spaniard.

In Spanish life, then, there is often this sense of the incomplete and the broken off, of things begun and never to be ended, of the wave curling back on itself. There must be an activity of which Spaniards never tire and for which they are always apt and willing, but I cannot name it. It is said that in the good old days the male section of the populace never tired of quarrelling about politics, but under the present régime this habit is in abeyance. From casual observation it might seem to be talk in general and indeed, hearing the wag of a Spanish tongue, one may well echo Benedict's wish for a horse with the speed of it and half so good a continuer. But the vast body of proverbs and aphorisms in the Spanish language suggests that even the impulse to communicate is intermittent. A fund of sententious clichés to fall back on surely points to long slack periods in the brains of such as use them. Conversations are sometimes held, especially among peasants, which amount more or less to a stringing together of these maxims so that there is really no need for anyone to think at all. One might suppose again that the Spaniard is inexhaustible in the pursuit and enjoyment of pleasure, for certainly he is prepared to exert himself in this field as in few others. The drawback is that there is not enough pleasure in Spain for the thesis to get a fair trial. While we marvel at the distances a boy will walk to a *fiesta*, the hours a girl will spend on her dress, the money that the poverty-stricken will find for a bull-fight, the patience of young and old as they wait for some very modest entertainment to begin, we have to set it all against the hard simplicities of their daily life. And in this last, in the words "patience" and "wait", is perhaps a clue to what we are looking for. It may be that Spaniards tire least of the very thing that occidentals as a rule find peculiarly irksome, even intolerable, which is to do nothing at all. I remember a Good Friday in the little Andalusian village of Benalmáddena where a miming of the Passion is held in the open every year. It was supposed to begin at half-past nine in the morning and the Roman legionaries and apostles began trickling towards the field at ten minutes to four, their movements calm and unhurried. Most Spaniards have an uncanny way of knowing or sensing when this kind of thing is going to happen, but on that day there were a fair number of them as well as foreigners. These latter stamped up and down and cursed, explored the village, took photographs, went walking or, as the day crept on, vanished into wineshops. The Spaniards sat quietly on small wooden chairs and gazed ahead. Only when some fellow countrymen, wilier than they, appeared at half-past three with chairs in their hands and set them down in front, blocking the view entirely, was there a wild beautiful burst of rage: otherwise they might have been in a trance. On that occasion, at least, they had something to look forward to but they behave no differently when they have not. As I have said, terrible things happen on local trains when bigger and faster ones are coming down the line: they are shunted ruthlessly on to sidings and rest there *perdus* by the hour, and as they get later and later more and more of the others naturally require the line, with indescribable confusion as a result. Nothing in the world is so bereft of life and hope as a Spanish local train in a siding. The sun glares down at its roof, and the passengers by drawing all the blinds down turn it into an oven: the station vendors of fruit or water seldom come out as far and officials shout untruthfully at would-be fugitives that it is just about to leave. I do not think I ever saw any Spanish man, woman or child show annoyance or irritation at such times. Friends of mine who once had a wait of nine suffocating hours outside Valencia report that the other passengers were calm and poised to the end. One time in Seville I sat in a coach that ought to have left for Cadiz an hour and a half previously, while the other passengers smoked and chatted in undertones. At last the driver put his head in and remarked, "This coach will not be going to-day," at which they placidly took up their belongings and got out. I have often wondered how long they would have sat before it occurred to someone to make inquiries if the driver had not come at all.

This exemplary behaviour may be partly due of course to something other than torpor or even fatalism, namely, to the dread of appearing ridiculous. Nothing can well be more absurd than the spectacle of a man fretting and fuming over what cannot be helped, but the highly pitched northerner will often forgo his dignity to enjoy the happiness and relief of explosion. This is incredible to the Spaniard, whose idea of himself is only equalled in importance to him by the *figura* he wishes to cut in the eyes of others. Displays of feeling other than anger, in certain conditions, or gallantry or love for children tend not merely to diminish the *figura* but to endanger it by giving its secrets away. Donne's contention that no man is an island would find little echo in Spanish hearts, for the

Spaniard regards himself as just that, a very special and indeed unique island but one that is perpetually threatened and in need of fortification: not bristling with guns, as unsteady egoisms are apt to do with us, but fitted with an impenetrable shell to retire behind at the first alarm. This characteristic is often compared to the Oriental and Irish need of "face" but in fact differs from it in a most important particular. Face-saving is a mere keeping-up of appearances whether they deserve it or not, while the *figura* needs an inner truth to sustain it. Thus, for instance, while an Irishman may rob without mercy or shame and yet be thoroughly put out if anyone calls him a thief, the Spaniard likes the *figura* he offers the world to be substantial enough to convince himself. It will often compel him to be more generous or brave or virtuous than is natural or convenient: we might, if feeling out of sorts, put the whole thing down to a kind of vanity, but not to an ignoble kind.

The Spaniard then will betray no emotion in the most hideous circumstances lest somebody should suppose him to be made of flesh and blood; and he will be more than usually stony if foreigners are present, for otherwise it might be taken as an admission that something in Spain was less than perfect. But when all the allowances are made for this endearing trait, it still is true that immobility and inertia weary him less than the other people in western Europe. Consider the Spanish ability to sleep at any time and in any place, how the old women will drowse an afternoon away in doorways with people continually pushing and nudging and stepping over them, how youths stretch out on station benches with loco-motives screeching a few yards from their ear, how at *fiestas* small children sleep untroubled in their mothers' arms through the deafening roar that only Spanish fireworks can make. A Spaniard apparently has only to stay in the one position for a while to slip off into oblivion, so that sleep would appear, as with lions, to be their habitual state. The baffling thing is that constitutionally they seem hardly to require any sleep at all, as those who have travelled through the night in a Spanish train or tossed and turned on a hotel bed with voices booming under their window from cock crow to sunrise will agree. They may not need it, but still they must love it for its interruption to the terrible business of living.

❧ 9 ❧

AND AS THE INDIVIDUAL DOZES FOR HALF A DAY THE race will doze for a couple of centuries and more. Time and again as one goes about the country one has the sense that nothing has been done here for hundreds of years. Spain is not "unspoiled" so much as unchanged: we see things continually that can hardly have looked different to Cervantes or Teresa de Jesús or El Greco, to the Catholic kings and the *conquistadores*, the poets and singers of the *siglo de oro*. Not merely buildings and landscapes are the same but people and what they do, the woman coming from the well with the earthen jar on her head, the peasant tending his ancient olives or vines, the girl perched so casually behind the horseman on their way to the *romería*, the hooded penitents of the *cofradías*, the young boy who minds the sheep or goats on the lonely mountainside and half expects the Virgin to appear. Some years ago a company filmed *La Vida de Lazarillo de Tormes*, the sixteenth-century anonymous tale of a boy living on his wits among the beggars, priests, nobles and villains of Salamanca and Toledo, which was the first of the Spanish picaresque novels and often thought to be the best. It was astonishing how little it dated in situation or atmosphere or, above all, in humour, the Spaniards being as slow to abandon a good joke as anything else that appeals to them: and the scenes from street, presbytery, market-place or church in the two cities are more or less as we may find them ourselves to-day.

Particularly is this true of Toledo which exhales the sense of things gone by in the way that Ragusa does, or Venice: it is a flake of history, the little city crowning a hill with a river curled about it like a green snake, and looking just as it did in the paintings of El Greco. Here there is a little of everything that went to the making of Spain. The feel of the Zoco is Moorish with the baked sandy walls and colonnade and the rounded arch framing a view of faraway red earth and dark little trees. Moorish and Jewish also are many of the faces of the men and women passing through it: there is a flashing reptilian something in the eyes, a something far from benignant and an unSpanish mobility of expression. Indeed there is a strongly semitic flavour to Toledo as a whole. The dealers lurking in the myriad little souvenir shops go to such lengths to coax the tourist inside and hold him there that it might be Tangier or Port Said; and each of them will gravely warn his victim against the others. But the core of it is the old cathedral, towering over all, the sudden appearance of whose spire against the sky at our journey's end is as thrilling whether we see it for the twentieth time or the first.

Toledo in summer is wonderfully hot: I am always forgetting how hot and intending to do things there for which, when it comes to the point, the flesh is too weak. When last I arrived, however, a fierce summer rain was lashing down as if trying to put out a fire and the citizens, cat-like, had all fled indoors. It went on raining all through the night and the morning air was deliciously cool, so that I leaped out of bed determined to do all manner of improving things. Every morning in the mozarab chapel of the cathedral the Eastern Rite is celebrated, a curiosity that many intend to see once and as a rule never do: that was to be the first place of call. The chapel was in the Moorish style, unkempt and forlorn, remote from the others and empty except for me. Priests kept dashing through to a sacristy behind, slamming the heavy doors or gossiping noisily outside, as if they objected to the alien ritual being carried out in the first cathedral of Spain. Their behaviour was a contrast to the reverence and utter absorption in his task of the celebrant, a man with the face and hands of a saint by El Greco, such as I never before had seen. Spain teems with Velázquez faces and Goya faces, but a true El Greco face is rare and is quite likely to belong to a Frenchman anyhow: so that there was a great charm in the scene, the candlelight falling on the calm oval face and hollow eyes, the beautiful fingers turning the pages, the murmur of the voice, the man's air of peace and detachment, with never so much as a glance at the naughty little buffoon who acted as server.

Well, that was that: I was no wiser or better, but still there was the bizarre glee of the tourist as he ticks something off the agenda. High Mass was beginning now and priests of all shapes and sizes and degrees of eminence were pouring raggedly towards their stalls. The ritual was carried out in the slovenly manner habitual in Spain and while the faithful received communion the organist was merrily playing Debussy's *Jeune Fille aux Cheveux de Lin*. No doubt Spaniards are so profoundly spiritual and religious that decorum and beauty in worship strike them as a frill, or even a snare, rather in the way that saints and holy men might frown on the use of soap and water. Gabbling priests, rowdy acolytes, grubby vestments, candles drunkenly reeling and raining grease on all around, flowers faded or dead, statues thick with dust, sacristans spitting on the floor, are more the rule than the exception and Toledo can hold its own with any. Yet the grandeur of the old cathedral itself throws a kind of dignity over all that happens there, even to the huckstering in the cloisters. The place is a jumble of magnificence and beauty and squalor and neglect. The grime on the immensely ornate High Altar is somehow touching, as if the fervent souls who raised it up had been so busy piling riches on riches that they forgot how impossible it would be to keep it clean.

Here in Toledo there is an adorable Mother and Child, one of the radiant ones that do exist in Spain among all the skulls and scourges and painted wounds and tears of glass: my favourite of them all, this, preferred even to that enchanting pair at the Cartuja in Granada, Risueño's Virgin of the Rosary with the *Niño alegre*. There is a touch of Kwannon's calm benevolence in this Madonna with the long narrow eyes and smiling lips: no hint of sorrow to come disturbs the lovely brow: the infant in her arms is stroking her under the chin and looking impishly to see how she likes it. All here is sweetness and joy and repose, so that it need hardly be said the faithful do not readily flock to her, any more than they do to Our Lady of Joy in Barcelona, who is thought so little of that she has to share her chapel with Pio X.

I was feasting my eyes on her when a hammering of indescribable vehemence broke out, like some proletarian symphony in praise of honest toil. It shook the very brain in one's skull, although the Spaniards kneeling all round in prayer never so much as looked up. I took to my heels and went down to the Zocodover in search of breakfast and entertainment. The cafés there were every bit as piratical as of yore but the square brimmed with life as ever and was well worth the twenty per cent or so clapped on the bill. There was some little hint of progress in the blue government van with the loudspeaker that bellowed like a bull and described its function as *Servicio de Extensión Cultural*, but none whatever in the bunch of old peasants who looked at it and muttered with scepticism written large on their scorched and wrinkled faces. Slender young officers from the Alcázar were strolling in twos and threes with a click of spur and jingle of sword. Later in the day perhaps they would have to exchange their elegant uniform for a shiny cotton suit and go to another humbler sphere to keep body and soul together: a sad business, for when a Spaniard puts uniform off a kind of shrinking and withering takes place, as with a pierced balloon. Now there came that old rascal in excessively national garb with his *burro* heaped and slung about with Toledo pottery, for sale at extortionate rates. A feature of Spanish economy worth noting is that prices are often fixed in inverse proportion to overheads: the rustic pedlar and the kerb market are to be eschewed, therefore, despite their appeal and we should rather proceed to a big shop in a fashionable street. The pedlar now stationed himself as near to the best café as the waiters would allow and began to sing his wares in a nasal whine, while the *burro* stood switching his flanks with a meagre tail and looking unutterably sardonic, as if he knew what he knew but preferred not to speak. Two blind men were crossing the Zoco from opposite ends, two out of the hosts of afflicted that strike another oriental note in Toledo. Halfway across they blundered into each other and one of them, who did not realize that the other was blind too, showered curses on him as he stood there with a terrible smile on his face, a grim rueful ironic compassionate smile that made the heart turn over.

The morning could have slipped away before these little incidents and spectacles began to pall, but I was still in a serious frame of mind and, having finished breakfast and argued the bill as an empty but soothing ritual act, I went in search of El Greco. The Museo Vicente was shut, a woman called from a door near by: but let me come along and she would show handmade lace at bargain prices. At what hour would the museum open? It would not open again, it was to be closed for ever: how about a Toledan sabre, or a *damasquino* tortoise? Or I might like to come and watch *damasquino* being made, no one would molest me if I didn't buy. Had the fifteen El Greco paintings gone to the Prado, or where? No, they were all inside still, quite safe: why should they go anywhere? Foreigners thought of nothing but El Greco. It was El Greco this and El Greco that with them all the time, *ay Señora! pero mire,* she had scissors and fans to offer as well as lace or a tortoise. . . .

How very Spanish of Spain to get up to her tricks on a cool silvery morning that put one of itself in the mood for El Greco! It happens so often, this apparently capricious withholding of masterpieces from the public eye: to some extent made up for by the fact that in out of the way corners you frequently stumble on treasures that no one has bothered to mention, but none the less infuriating. "Often when you have toiled through the heat and dust to some distant church, museum, library, or what not, after much ringing and waiting, you will be drily informed that it is shut, can't be seen, that it is the wrong day, that you must call again to-morrow; and if it be the right day, then you will be told that the hour is wrong, that you are come too early, too late; very likely the keeper's wife will inform you that he is out, gone to mass, or market, or at his dinner, or at his *siesta*, or if he is at home and awake, he will swear that his wife has mislaid the key, 'which she is always doing'." The words are those of the incomparable Richard Ford and are as true to-day as in 1846: the same can be said of much that he wrote and we have only to open the *Gatherings from Spain* at any page to find talk of things we have seen our-selves, described far better than we could have done it, which is salutary but dispiriting. But a long appreciative study of the master backed by years of wandering about the country have somehow failed to teach me sense, and like any beginner I went down to the *Oficina de Turismo* to ask for the truth. It had, as sole regent this morning, a boy of about twelve with beautiful manners and the dignity of a Bedouin sheikh. He greeted me as an old friend, for we had met on my previous visit. Then I was looking into the chances of getting to La Mancha by road or rail from Toledo without becoming a physical and nervous wreck on the way. All at once the notion took me to see El Toboso in blazing midsummer, with the windmills and the sheep and the great serene luminous clouds sailing over the sky. The infant let me ramble on with perfect composure, meditated briefly, consulted a textbook and then, delivering himself like an oracle, urged me to return at once to Madrid and start from there. That first short meeting had been constrained: neither of us could relax. I thought that children should not have such heavy duties laid upon them and he believed no good would come of foreign women wandering about in La Mancha. None the less it had paved the way to a cordial understanding now. The boy did not share the tradeswoman's view of El Greco at all. He said that he was the greatest painter who had ever lived and that his greatest pictures were all here in Toledo: not in Madrid, as people often supposed. On hearing that the Vicente was shut he studied the official leaflet with a puzzled frown and then, cheering up, showed where it gave the museum's address and opening hours. "It cannot be shut," he explained, "it is on our list." Nothing could shake him in this simple faith, nor would he discuss the matter further. He rummaged about in the dusty shelves and with a triumphant smile produced another leaflet, this time in French, which listed the Vicente again. Then he took pencil and paper and with childish concentration, knuckles white, tongue licking upper lip, drew a plan of how to get there.

No doubt of it, my friends the *Kunsthistoriker* in London would know if the Vicente were shut or not: they always know everything. The rational and speediest way of finding out was to write to them and await their reply. Meanwhile there were the busy squares and lanes to ramble, one of the finest occupations known to man. I can think of no pleasanter way of spending a morning than simply to wander about alone in search of no particular thing, merely accepting and enjoying whatever may turn up. But Spaniards cannot abide to see people wandering about alone: it both annoys and disquiets them. It may perhaps be due to the great stretches of vacuity and desolation in their country, but they must always be snuggling down together and in their need for reassurance far prefer unsuitable company to none. The words "far from the madding crowd" would make no sense to them at all. For one thing, every little event however trivial must be talked over with someone at once, otherwise it does not seem to have really happened. So that in no time at all I was accompanied, first by five or six little boys who were exceedingly anxious

that we should all go fishing in the Tagus together, then by
two giggling girls in the severe blue and white uniform of a
convent, then by a student who wished to practise his English
and boast of his female conquests at one and the same time
and finally by a tenacious old man in brown corduroys who
told me that he was a Catalan. He stuck to me like a limpet for
an hour and a half. Although more than fifty years of his life
had been spent in Toledo he had not come round to it at all.
The Toledans, he told me, were completely barbarous and
ignorant and without any outside interest, so that it was painful
for a man like himself to have to associate with them. Cataluña,
on the other hand, was the heart, force and intellect of Spain.
The Catalans were people of culture and eager to converse with
foreigners, in order to learn about the world outside and to
enlarge their minds. When it came down to brass tacks, however, he spoke only about himself. He had three fixed beliefs
to which in conversation he always returned, namely, that he
spoke perfect French, that he was descended from Christopher
Columbus and that everyone who knew him loved him; and
one can only hope the second two were better founded than
the first. He came down the hill as far as the Puerta del Sol, his
jaws working indefatigably, and then declared he must go and
buy vegetables for his dinner. He shook my hand repeatedly,
and hinted that a little *propina* would be acceptable. After all,
one did not meet the descendants of Christopher Columbus
every day.

Now the sun was beginning to reassert itself and the gardens
beyond the Puerta de Bisagra were cool and green and inviting.
Along the benches under the high leafy plane trees the eternal
grey old men were nodding and dozing with mangy dogs
nosing the dust around their feet for crumbs. The zany house
of cork was locked and shuttered as if people were tired of the
joke. Orphans swarmed in the courtyard of the Tavera Hospital, shrieking at the top of their lungs while the guardian of
the Museo slept among them, his peaked cap over his eyes, his

head pillowed on a block of stone. There is a deadening ring to the very word *Museo* and I avoid such places unless there are pictures in them. That morning for some reason I stepped over the recumbent form of the *custode* and rang the bell. A frail blue-eyed old gentleman answered it and led the way inside, to what in fact was the Duchess of Lerma's Toledo house and open to the public only when she was away. The rooms were long and bare with a few fine pictures and pieces in each with the characteristic blend of austerity and splendour: the long rough dining-board cut from one piece of wood, polychrome statues, glass paintings, coffers, candlesticks, brocades gave the sense of a family continuing grandly down the centuries. The archives of Cardinal Tavera's Hospital from the time of its founding were all kept in the library, a medley of letters from the king and other great personages of the day, notes for grain received from the lands, bills from El Greco and Berruguete for work done about the place. There was a portrait of the Cardinal founder, a true mediaeval churchman with his bleak grey face, which had marks in the canvas showing where it was repaired after a mob had torn it to pieces in the Civil War; and one by Ribera, of a bearded peasant woman from the Abruzzi that, with a Spanish taste for the horrific, the Duke of Alcalá had commissioned while he was Viceroy of Naples. Difficult to live with, it might have been supposed, that lined mannish face and flowing black beard above the round white breast giving suck to an uncritical baby; but the old gentleman accompanying me lingered over it with affection, chuckling with delight. He seemed to be one of the family, he took such pride and pleasure in everything and asked with such fervour if the portrait of the last Duchess were not *"guapísima"*, as indeed it was. The rooms of the present Duchess had the characteristic mingling of grandeur and simplicity too, and a general effect as if the lady were somewhat amused by her own eminence. In one room there was a portrait of her husband as a handsome young man: he was shot in the Civil War, and her son killed as well. Afterwards she gave a house to the orphans of the war without political discrimination. The portrait brought the tale of tragedy and generosity back again and turned the palace, with its curious air of waiting and listening that very old houses have, into a moving, very significant place: it seemed as it stood now, empty and unused, to draw attention composedly to the end of an old order, while the yells of the happy and nameless swarming in the courtyard below heralded a new.

The old gentleman opened the door to the gateway, trembling like a leaf, one more of the numberless shaky old guardians of Spain. The sun was completely in force by now and licked up the puddles of rain as if it were dying of thirst. The heavy scent of wilting roses hung in the air; the river was green no longer but tawny, like the eyes of a cat. It may be hotter in Seville or Merida but in Toledo one has the feeling of being specially picked out and put under the grill, like a steak in a good restaurant: the old Spanish belief that the sun shone on Toledo first in all creation is very natural, and for aught I know may be true. The sky that two hours before had been so fresh and moist and dull was blazing like a furnace. My resolution crumbled away and I went back to the hotel for luncheon and a *siesta*. A horde of Germans had descended on it and, with faces the colour of boiled prawns, were doggedly munching their way through the long *prix fixe* – "es ist doch bezahlt!" – before being hounded off to another dose of culture. As usual, the lift was not working. All through the torrid afternoon a girl in the street below leaned against a doorway and sang a snatch of *flamenco* over and over, just the same seven or eight notes, over and over again. I wanted to shoot her until a Frenchwoman in the room next to mine began angrily expostulating and then I longed to shoot her instead, an irate French voice being infinitely more tedious than *flamenco* could ever be.

Spain is the land of orphans: how or why I do not know, but apparently there are more orphans even than religious. Point to any large building and ask what it is and two to one you will hear that it is an orphanage. This fact of Spanish life obtruded itself once more in the evening as I was deep in the contemplation of El Greco's "Funeral of the Conde Orgaz" in Santo Tomé and a crowd of giggling little girl orphans was shepherded in by a nun. She wore the blue habit of Vincent de Paul and her face under the white folds of her cap was like an old apple; having installed her little charges in the rows of chairs facing the picture she sat down to one side of it with a groan of pleasure and at once dozed off. A guide stepped forward and began a speech that I had often heard before and that probably never would vary whether addressed to artists, orphans, scholars, honeymoon couples or, indeed, to El Greco himself. The little girls chewed gum, whispered, poked each other, scratched their heads and looked everywhere but at the masterpiece: the upward flowing lines of whose composition, the guide informed them, expressed in a perfect manner the soaring spirituality of the immortal and sublime Toledan genius. This guide was not of the good old traditional sort with the bristly chins and villainous breath but a real *señorito* with oily hair and tiny moustache, clad in a white shirt and blue trousers and utterly delighted with himself: as long as he could harken to the rise and fall of his own tenor voice he did not seem to care if his audience were with him or not. The instant his harangue came to an end the old nun woke up, as if to a pre-arranged signal; and having rewarded him modestly and led her flock in a few gabbled Aves before the altar, ushered the chewing and giggling little monkeys out of the church, no doubt greatly improved and enriched by the experience.

The incursion of all these explosive little beings had made a further enjoyment of the painting impossible and I went beyond the city walls for a walk. Walking is not the pleasant and easy thing in Spain that it is at home: time and again one meets with magnificent open country only to find there are no paths through to it, or paths that go a little way and stop short, or paths that lead up to a house whence a large cross dog will rush out, or even to barricades of barbed wire. It is natural enough, for no Spaniard goes merely walking: he would think such a proceeding insane. A Spaniard on foot is a Spaniard going from A to B for a definite purpose, and who cannot afford a car. He assumes that this is true of everyone else and it makes for new difficulty. In his goodness he will come after you as at last you turn down a path that seems headed for the wild and will cry, "Excuse me! that is not the way to the *parador*." But you are not going to the *parador*. "Then you will be going to the Casa Blanca, and in that case you have come too far." It ends with him standing rooted to the ground and staring after you in bewilderment and disapproval.

Again, Spanish walks frequently end in utter exhaustion, particularly when they have included a short cut. Two or three miles up the road that leads from Toledo past the Cigarral Monte Rey there is a steep goat-path that winds away from the hill and drops to the side of the river. In lunatic optimism I climbed down this, hoping the river there would be low enough in summer to wade across and save me the two or three miles of dusty *carretera*. But far from it, it was foaming and swirling and only waiting for something to swallow up; and having brought me to its brink the goat-path apparently considered its duty done and broke off. The choice was between retracing my steps, a mean and spiritless solution, or trying to scramble over the rocks as far as the weir and trying to wade over that. Voices were raised in a shout as I scaled the first boulder, whether in deprecation or encouragement it was hard to say. The geological make-up of the region was notable in that the boulders were either razor-sharp and sliced and grated the skin from arms and legs, or so smooth and round that one slid off them as if buttered. Why, I mused, clinging to a ledge three feet above the roaring current while my foot tremulously felt for a purchase somewhere, why do all this? It seemed to me at that moment as if all the time I had ever spent in this diabolical country had been passed in similar exercises. Voices shouted again and turning as best I could in their direction I saw a little further up one of the most familiar and Spanish and beautiful of scenes. A line of fishermen were standing across the weir with wide straw hats on their heads, knee-deep in water which ribbed out each side of them before it tumbled into the frothing pool below. Beyond the weir itself was a green island with children playing on it and a goat or two, and quiet shallow pools inshore that reflected the evening sky. Above it all was the lovely little city, peach-coloured in the dying sun, balanced so lightly and firmly on its rocky base and offering me in my present situation an entirely new aspect of itself, fresh detail of spire and arch and winding lane as well as a novel, exquisite whole. And only the moment before I had been wondering why I was there! O ye of little faith . . . Not only was I, stuck to my ledge like a limpet, rewarded with a sight of rare beauty but at last I was able to enjoy beauty in Spain at leisure, at peace and in solitude: our deepest prayers are always granted, although the manner of granting may sometimes amaze us.

Night had fallen when I reached Toledo again and under moon and stars and street lamps it had undergone a happy change. For the time being, the commercial frenzy had died away. The tourists had been borne off by coach and car and the Toledanos were relaxing and restoring themselves for the fresh blood of the morrow. The windows of the *damasquino* shops, so paltry by day, were all ashine and aglitter, a romantic haze of burnished silver and gold. The cathedral was lying in its orb of light with darkness all round, like a vision of peace and glory that some old monk of the Middle Ages might have had as he starved in his wretched cell. Women were sitting about on chairs in the open air, fanning themselves and moaning about the heat, and the popular cafés in the little streets and out-of-the-way squares were full of workmen shouting and smoking. At the top of the lane leading up from the

Zocodover was the Alcázar of immortal memory. There was great heroism on both sides in the Civil War, and great wickedness, and only the Recording Angel can say which had the more of either: nor are Spanish officers by any means the only ones in the world to put their duty before all else. But the story of the Alcázar, with the obstinate maintaining of routine, appearance and discipline, the holding of parades, the brave little celebration of the Feast of the Assumption, under constant bombing and shelling and on a diet of coarse bread and horsemeat, up to the day of the final unhoped-for deliverance, sounds a peculiarly Spanish note from beginning to end. We need only think of the laconic exchange between the commander of the garrison, Colonel Moscardó, and his son, when the lad's Republican captors brought him to the telephone. "What is happening, my boy?" "Nothing. They say they will shoot me if the Alcázar does not surrender." "If it be true, commend your soul to God, shout Viva España! and die like a hero. Good-bye, my son, a last kiss." "Good-bye, father, a very big kiss."[1] It may be said that *un beso muy fuerte* is a phrase any Spanish boy could normally use to his father when telephoning. As is well known, the garrison did not surrender and after a time the young man was shot. A Spaniard's children are "flesh of his flesh" in a way that his wife seldom is, while the agony of the son may be imagined; but it was not merely the greatness of the sacrifice that was so truly Spanish, it was also the mixture of sublime and matter-of-fact in the few little words that passed between the two. "Qué pasa, chico?" "Nada . . ." One cannot object to the reconstitution of the Alcázar. All over the country to-day there are shrines and memorials to perpetuate the legend of the "glorious crusade" and the name of the *señorito* founder of the Falange is painted

[1] Cf. Hugh Thomas, *The Spanish Civil War*, Eyre and Spottiswoode. There have been attempts to discredit this story by Spanish Republicans and liberals. The weight of the evidence supports it, however, and impartial people (in so far as such exist) mostly accept it. If it is not true, it ought to be; it is in keeping with Spanish tradition from Roman days on.

on the walls of nearly every church: only that unyielding old
war-horse the late Cardinal Segura of Seville declared the
practice contrary to canon law and, alone of the Spanish
hierarchy, forbade it. Those with any memory of the facts or
knowledge of what the "crusade" led to can hardly see them
without impatience, but the Alcázar is a different case. It stands
for another point of view than that which predominates in
Toledo now and is a reminder to it and to us that the precious
things of Spain are not only cathedrals and castles but ways of
thinking and doing that are older still. The new and far from
handsome building is therefore worthy of a visit; and night is
the best time to pay it.

❧ *IO* ❧

IT IS ODD HOW MANY PEOPLE WILL SAY THAT THEY
love Spain but do not care for Madrid. On examination it often
turns out that by Madrid they mean their hotel, Chicote's Bar,
the Gran Via and the Post Office, particularly the Post Office.
That dire specimen of the Wedding Cake school of architecture
certainly lodges in the mind and overcasts the memory. It is
not only ugly but enormous, partly because inside it, as in all
such edifices up and down the country, three men are doing
the work of one and requiring the space for it. The organization is, consequently, what we may expect: whole mornings
can be spent over a simple task like getting a packet off by air,
and some of the customers look as if they had lived there for
years.

Let me not, however, be swept off course so early in the
day by traumatic experiences of the past: nor, blinded by love,
attempt a specious defence of either the Gran Via or Chicote's.
It may be that a taste for Madrid is rather a special one, and it
is certain that Madrid is a special kind of capital. It has never,
for one thing, been granted the status of *ciudad*, city, but
remains simply a *villa*, town, while some old-fashioned people
still refer to it as the *Corte*, or Court. It has no real cathedral
of its own, although an enormous one has been in the process
of building for many a long year. While waiting for its com-
pletion, Madrid has used the church of San Isidro Labrador
in the Calle de Toledo, San Isidro being the patron of both
Court and town. This interesting saint, a poor agricultural
labourer, was born in the twelfth century and was married to

another saint, Maria de la Cabeza. The two of them agreed after some years of married life to separate and live in different places, for the sake of greater holiness. Many of the miracles wrought by San Isidro in his lifetime consisted of calling down heavenly forces to do his work for him, so that the title *Labrador* is perhaps not altogether descriptive; but he has a fine musty old church, containing many rich treasures, built by the Jesuits a few years after his canonization in 1622.

There is also no Opera House, such as one would expect to find in a European capital: it too waits to be built and it will be interesting to see whether Cathedral or Opera makes it first, or whether it will end in a dead heat. Theatres are plentiful, but confine themselves mostly to *flamenco*, mild domestic comedies, translations of old French or English hits and the perennial *zarzuelas*, or musical comedies. To say the Spanish theatre is a living force would be to overstate. And apart from architectural and cultural gaps, Madrid has no immediately obvious point to it. The centre of religion is Saragossa, where Our Lady appeared to St James on a marble pillar at the river edge and caused, among much else, huge numbers of Spanish girls to be called Pilar ever since; and Saragossa is closely rivalled by Santiago de Compostela, where the Apostle himself turned up in miraculous fashion and was buried, and by Toledo, the see of the Spanish Primate. For academic learning we must go to Salamanca, for business and general liveliness to Barcelona, for pleasure to Granada and Seville. What with one thing and another, we can understand the foreigner with his mind on gipsy dancers, Moorish remains and orange trees in flower complaining that this is not what he has come to Spain for, particularly as the time he usually allots to it is three days and that is barely long enough to suck the juice from a single room in the Prado.

None the less, one can hardly love Spain and not Madrid because Madrid is the core of Spain and Spanishness in an earthy way, just as Avila is in a spiritual. What king but a Spanish one, and even of Spanish kings which but the mulish Philip II, would have set up his Court at all in conditions of such magnificent inconvenience? Stuck in a desert, alternately scorched and frozen, on a river that is barely more than a stream for much of the year, equally far from the humanizing Mediterranean and the invigorating Atlantic, girt about by unwelcoming mountains. The gaunt Sierras that are so mysteriously beautiful from a roof-top in the evening light have barred the way to much. But these very drawbacks were what appealed to Philip II the most, and once the king had made up his mind there was no more to be said. *Yo el Rey*: there is something superbly arrogant and intractable in the very signature of the old Spanish monarchs.

As well as being in a figurative sense the core of Spain, Madrid is actually the heart of it. The central point is supposed to be the little old castle, perched on a base of natural rock a few miles out along the road to Segovia which gave its name to the Arab village of Torrelodones near by. In and around Madrid you get an idea of the contrasts and variety of Spanish land and people. A short drive will bring you up from the formal parks and avenues of the town to the bleak pine-covered Sierra where the car may stick on the frozen road and where blizzards are liable to occur any time up to the end of April. The last time I went there the forest was crawling with dignified Roman soldiers and grubby Goths: it was only Mr Sam Bronston again, directing the fall of the Roman Empire, but the creatures looked very much at home. On through the forest the road winds to fetch up at La Granja, summer residence of monarchs, which, squat and beturreted at the end of a little avenue formed by two rows of yellow-walled outhouses with trees in front, is so Austrian in appearance as to be really startling. A drive no longer in the other direction brings you to the warmth and southern vegetation of Aranjuez. It takes roughly the same time to reach the Sierra de Gredos, region of wild boar and wolves and salmon rivers, as to the immense vineyards on the baking slopes of Valdepeñas.

So there the capital is, easier of access in our day, newish as the towns of Spain go, fast building and filling up, containing nearly as many people as are in the whole province around. Up to now they have been spared the expanding belts of meanness that girdle the larger towns of France and England. Madrid is inclined to stop short, violently, capriciously, as if to say "that's that", in the way we might expect. In summer the Royal Palace looks out over a sea of ruffling tree-tops and even when the leaves are down the high salmon-coloured blocks springing up all over the *vega* beyond have an air of being put there just for the time being. Rocky spiky countryside may begin after a drive of twenty minutes, and this country flows into the city when the mood takes it: a peasant will push a cart of newly mown grass down the Gran Via or serenely ride his *burro* there as if he were in his village, and until a short time ago herds of goats and flocks of sheep driven by small boys would trip across the Puerta del Sol and along the Alcalá on Wednesday mornings. Sitting over a late Spanish breakfast in La Tropical or Le Lion d'Or one became aware of a light pattering, as of rain on leaves, and looking up would find hundreds of the little creatures streaming past, perfectly at their ease and aware of their rights, while the police looked on with benevolence and the traffic respectfully waited.

If this charming practice had not come to an end I would feel like voting it the epitome of Madridness. Every loved city has a scene or flavour or habit which seems peculiarly of itself and springs to the memory first. In Paris, for me, it is the smell of the Métro: not, as might indicate a higher degree of culture, the Sainte Chapelle or the bookstalls along the river or the *bistrot* where Jean-Paul Sartre holds court, but the smell of the Métro in all its variety from the fragrance of hot metal and grimy wet stone in the early morning to the voluptuous banks of garlic and wine during the post-prandial *heure d'affluence*.

And this touch of *rus in urbe*, the animals pouring along the fashionable street, the plaintive sound of their bells, the shepherd boys in beret and muffler, the grave men of Madrid in their formal grey or black looking on from the cafés while their shoes were cleaned, the early sun falling on the pinkish façade of the little Church of Las Calatravas, epitomized and called up the Spanish capital for me in the same way.

The Moorish Bodyguard has been done away with too, or that might almost have taken its place. There was a superb magnificence about those Moors, as they rode haughtily through the city of the conqueror without a glance to left or right. The dark faces under helmets spiked and turbaned, the voluminous white cloaks, the delicate lances held in the thin brown hands, reminded one of Saracens in old picture books about the Crusades. The hooves of their fiery mounts were washed gold and there was a stirring clatter and jingle of accoutrement as they swept by: their very trot seemed to have an African *brio* of its own. Sometimes an added touch of fairy-tale would be imparted by the State coach, gaudy, creaky, rumbling along in their midst with a plumed and brocaded Ambassador inside it. And one of the bodyguard was always on duty at the gates of the Pardo, the palace outside Madrid where General Franco lives: hour upon hour the man would sit, a still white figure on a motionless horse, rifle across knee, with a background of ochre-coloured earth and dark stunted trees, under a blazing blue sky. There was a harsh and splendid something in the scene, with an echo from far-off desert and mountains: one thought of bugles and moonlight ambushes and brave cunning young Franco sitting tight amid hordes of rebels and holding his own. Now Morocco is free, which is good, and the guard is gone, which is sad: progress and dullness often appear to be wedded.

Plenty is left, however, that speaks of Madrid and nowhere else. We might pick on something with a roof in it. Roofs are immensely important and nobody without access to one has a right to hold opinions of Madrid at all. A roof alters the entire conception at once. From the ground the city is grey or white, tall, forbidding, angular, with pools of deep shadow all round: it is definitely northern and bears the imprint of Hapsburg and Bourbon. Look upwards and far overhead there is a narrow strip of blue with sunshine yellowing the tops of the houses, and you are surprised to remember that somewhere up above is the Spanish day. From the roof there is a maze of warm rosy or honey-coloured tiles, southern, almost Andalusian in feeling, slumbering and shimmering in the heat, with the magnificent land of Castile encircling it. It is on the roof that the garden is laid out, the tubs of petunia, rose, lilac and honeysuckle, the sparse crop of peas and beans, the attenuated tomato. The innocent blue-brown eyes of a rabbit peer from a hutch, a little pig is grunting. A friend of mine tried to rear ducklings, but they all died of shock on being introduced to a pool with rubber sides. The crowing of cocks at dawn in the heart of Madrid is one of its charming sounds, like the clapping of hands for the watchman at night. In the cool of the evening there is the delicious custom of *tomando el fresco* in comfortable chairs, while we rake all other roof-owners with a practised eye and talk over the events of the day. Talking and watching are about the only two things that Spaniards care to do simultaneously.

Or we might choose something watery, for water here has a special, almost a holy, significance, like money. The fountains lit from within are charming on a summer night, with their amber glow and the cool hiss of their spray. Less poetic but quite as typical are the scenes daily enacted by water in its domestic capacity. A scalding jet issues from the tap marked *Frío*, an orange gush leaves behind it a rich alluvial deposit down the middle of the bath or a derisive gurgle betokens that there is to be no water at all. That gurgle mocks and comforts at once in a manner peculiar to Spain, sneering at the hot dusty traveller who dared take something for granted and in the same breath giving a *¡bienvenido a Madrid!* more subtle than flowers could be: and a strange inward pleasure joins with the melancholy as you sponge down with the brackish residue from some water-bottle.

There are times when it is difficult not to believe that Spain is under the management of demons. One day the gurgle described above greeted me as after many days of procrastination I had set about doing some laundry. Typical, I thought: the plumbing had somehow got wind of my plans. On leaving the flat, however, I learned that the whole house, the whole street and indeed the whole *barrio* was waterless. No one could explain it, although it was vaguely ascribed to the *obras* in progress all over Madrid, with gangs of men tunnelling fiercely everywhere like an army of moles, with such disloyal purpose and catastrophic effect that a young friend of mine declared them to be the residue of the anarchist movement, the sting, as it were, in the tail. There was an *obra* not a hundred yards away, it was true, but it had been there for years: why should it suddenly cut the water now? The *barrio* was a very good one and to understand what had happened one must suppose that all the water round Portland Place or The Boltons was suddenly turned off, without warning or apology, and that no one could or would say for how long. Also, that nobody complained: but perhaps that is asking too much of an English imagination.

Yet here too Spain took with one hand and gave with the other. As the hideous drought continued over night and into the next day, there was nothing for it but to go to a waterpoint in the park, carrying pots, pails, tubs, bottles or whatever came to hand. A mob of servant girls was already collected there, shrieking like jays, with a footman or two in striped pink waistcoats and a few young pages. The hour and a half that followed before my turn came round was, in spite of a freezing April wind, a time of undiluted pleasure and instruction. Spaniards do have an expression for queueing up, namely, *hacer la cola,* but the thing itself seems not to have taken any real hold in their minds. Appalling lies flowed from the maids' lips as they strove to reach the water sooner than was their right, a flow punctured with cries of *¡Qué barbaridad!* and enlivened with a little hand-to-hand fighting. A man in the brown corduroys and the green-cockaded hat of a park attendant came up with his clay water-bottle and by threatening to cut the water off altogether got to the head of the queue at once. Next two uniformed *policías armadas* strolled up in the assumption that they would get the same privilege, whereas the maids, all rancour forgotten, themselves instantly, entirely, united, turned on them and drove them off, revolvers and all. A determined Spanish woman of whatever class is a match for Army, Church and State. Now it was the turn of the little maid in the flat opposite to my friend's, who had been shivering there in her short sleeves and cotton dress for so much longer than I but would hear of nothing but that I should take her place; and so, frozen to the marrow, I stumbled thankfully away, my ears still ringing with the quips and ripostes of the adder-tongued madrileñas and my heart warmed by the memory of the two disconcerted policemen slinking off.

A sight to enchant you in Madrid is the *lamparista* with flaming spear going from one lamp to the next along the Recoletos as the last colour drains from the sky, and then the soft gaslight falling on the trees, making the foliage a peculiar velvety green. I inquire after the lamps every time I reach Madrid nowadays, for in the frenzy of *modernización* little is holy or safe and the lunatic dreams of multitudes would appear to be row upon row of arc lamps shedding their ghastly blue glare on all around until the city looks like the pirate's cave in a pantomime. Spanish friends are often vexed by this anxiety, being themselves awearied of stumbling about in semi-darkness and falling down shafts, traps or manholes that someone has forgotten to shut. "You don't have to live here," is their dry observation, and there is no answer. It is pleasant to be foreign anywhere, in Spain it is wellnigh essential.

The best way to look for Madrid, and indeed for anywhere at all, is to go on foot; but if it is too hot or if, men of our time, we have lost the use of our legs, undoubtedly the second best is by taxi. The cabmen of big cities seem to take on the flavour of them and the Madrileño driver has an added piquancy in that he seldom knows the capital well, so that anticipation is heightened by suspense. He is not blandly ignorant and indifferent as are many of the metropolitan police, but he is apt to be vague. The asperity with which he may greet a foreign client, so far removed from the gentleness of Italy or the polish of France, is in the main protective. This foreigner may well want to go somewhere unheard of and cause him to lose face. And something in his mind resists the aridity of the skeletal address: he wants you to make it live for him. Bid him drive to a street that he does not know and he will mumble peevishly over his guidebook until you threaten to get out and walk; but if you can add some little touch or detail to stir his fancy, such as "You know, where they found the headless girl last month," the stern face relaxes and he bowls you away in a twinkling.

The challenge this sternness offers and the creative effort to overcome it, so that the long search for the goal may end in total participation and absolute harmony, greatly add to the pleasures of the drive. And although you will be terrified in his company you will not be at all bored. If he talks he does it well, with a wry salty Castilian humour, and unless he thinks you want conversation, splendid fellow, he will hold his peace altogether. Except on one occasion. The terse command, *To the bulls!* will release a flow that nothing can dam, continuing in spate until the ring is reached and reluctantly he must set you down. Change and decay in the *corrida*, anecdotes of the vanished great, style and habits of the present, highlights of the season in progress, it all comes tumbling out as he drives

121

on, his face in profile so that one eye may fix the passenger while the other is available for the traffic; and at a certain moment he will confide that he ought to have been a *torero* himself, much as an Irishman in drink will disclose that Nature intended him for the priesthood.

The unquiet spirit, then, weary of the cinema-hoardings in the Gran Via and deeply hostile to the Post Office, may leave itself in his care as long as abstractions are avoided. Even to say "Show me Madrid" does not really do, for "Madrid" in that sense verges on the conceptual and he will react by driving up and down the Gran Via, with a look in at the Post Office. The approach he likes is "I want to see gardens, Spaniards, the old town, marionettes, or a fish-market": he wants his own taste, judgement, experience and knowledge to be enlisted, he craves to be allowed to put himself in the other person's place. Then he will do his utmost, imaginative and disinterested, unless professional zeal and artistic fervour should conflict with something that has priority. If asked finally to leave the fare at some attractive little restaurant of his own choosing, with a terrace or garden perhaps, Castilian specialities, good wine, well thought of but quiet, he is quite capable of whipping you off to a hot low-ceilinged dive that reeks of garlic, rank oil and tired *merluza*, and has a juke-box. This action is so utterly at variance with all his others as to constitute a mystery, the kind that travellers will brood on for months and even years until their picture of a whole land is gradually and ineffaceably coloured by it; and yet the truth, laughably simple, is that the dive in question belongs to a fourth or fifth cousin of your man, and all fares inquiring for places to eat in are implacably deposited there.

Even in high summer and with Madrid a furnace, however, the best way to know it is to wander about on foot, free to stare and marvel and ponder. Window-gazing is of the highest importance: the richness of Spanish life and the complexity of the Castilian character may be inferred by simply looking into shops. At home, for example, a good Men's Hatter is a restrained affair of black, brown or grey, predictable as to form and rebarbative as to change: a checked cloth cap is the limit to which exuberance may aspire, while a green Tiroler suggests that the firm is going downhill. But the *Sombrerero* of Madrid, what a profusion of colours and shapes and ideas, what a jostling of centuries and regions, how provocative the association of spiritual and temporal! The red hat of a Cardinal, imposing even in vacancy, has for neighbour the crash-helmet of a motor-cyclist; and beside that is the seventeenth-century black velvet bonnet with its crimson and yellow plume of an *alguacil*, the mounted constable who nowadays requests the key of the pen from the president of a bull-fight. There are rows of black *birettas* with their fat pompoms of red, green or purple beside the arrestingly vivid wear of Spanish golfers or marksmen: there are tall black hats for a funeral, glossy broad-brimmed black beavers for a secular priest, round black berets for a Basque peasant or bohemian foreign author, dull black hats with the characteristic bow front and squared behind for the *torero* and those of similar cut but shiny for the *Guardia Civil*. A hard wide hat of palest grey calls up a vision of lean burned men in tight trousers and high-heeled boots with spurs riding across the parched Cordoban plain. And often and often I have puzzled over the coquettish little velvet toques in rose madder, sapphire blue or emerald green, with the saucy point to the crown and the round bobbles, so apparently ill-suited to the long severe Castilian face. For a *majo*? a *maja*? What occasion in the life of the face's owner could such a headdress possibly mark? As usual, my Spanish friends do not know and cannot think why anyone should want to know. A clue seemed to offer itself when the Duchess of Alba wore one at the *Corrida Goyesca* in June 1961 while requesting the key; but that was a historic moment, the first time a woman had participated in, let alone led, the taurine ritual march to

123

the arena, and the Duchess may with aristocratic freedom have improvised her attire as the fancy took her.

There are numbers of photographers too, for no self-respecting Spaniard can ever be photographed too often. A remarkable feature of their windows is the large portraits of small children after First Communion, girls dressed as little brides, boys in the impressive uniform of some religious knighthood: rosaries are twined round the little gloved hands, the little faces turn skywards as if in a precocious longing for heaven. It all takes parent and photographer a long time to arrange, the goal being an expression of such spirituality that all eyes moisten on beholding it and a general murmur of *¡Qué angelito!* goes up. This too is worth noting, for not only are Spanish children fiends but their parents like them to be fiends. If a Spanish child were to stop being fiendish for a couple of hours the parents almost certainly would get him away to the sea. This dichotomy of aspiration and fact, of reality and myth, is one more Spanish constant to be borne in mind.

When exhaustion comes there are the cafés, full of Spaniards watching Spaniards and the harsh rumble of Spanish talk. Anyone reading a neswpaper is likely to be foreign, for the inhabitants do not waste their precious viewing-time in that way. They have the passionate interest in other people that is one of the Spaniard's most charming if sometimes inconvenient characteristics. Friends with whom I sometimes stay live on a tenth floor and it is impossible to get the lift without the collaboration of the lift-boys. The characteristic sound in this building is a hysterical ringing of bells on every floor, accompanied by shouts of anger or appeal, as the minutes pass and the lift stays grounded. The boys are out in the street, watching the people in that wholehearted Spanish way, oblivious of time, place and self; and once the choler of the moment is gone the tenants regard this as a proper and natural thing.

Recently I found a guide-book advising strangers who

wanted to see Madrid in comfort to sit in an open-air café and watch it go by. The broad and handsome Avenue Castellana, lined with fragrant acacia trees and thronged with people from all over Spain and the Spanish world, was suggested as particularly adapted to this end. The advice is kind and well-intentioned but, like much that guide-books say, it requires a footnote. Madrid and Spain and Spanish America stream down the Castellana all right but the inquiring stranger will be lucky if he gets an occasional glimpse of them. A living wall of men, deep in conversation, will almost certainly screen it from his view. Consideration for others postulates the knowledge that others exist, and Spaniards are not at all sure of that: thus we cannot fairly tax them with the want of it. It is something different, something deep in the Spanish male that urges him irresistibly to interpose himself between spectator and spectacle.

Sometimes those who wish to know what is happening in the street are goaded into holding a mirror above their heads. Others accept the position and simply look around them. The changes coming over the city and the whole country are reflected in the cafés which, except for one or two special places like the Gijón or the Cocodrilo, used to be entirely a venue for men. They had the peculiar quality that monasticism imparts, a mingling of the severe, the fraternal and the squalid, and were used for all manner of business purposes. Customers sat by the hour over one drink, arguing or writing or simply hatching schemes, waiters took messages, ran errands and gave advice as well as waiting: the uncalled-for entry of a woman gave rise to frowning and staring. But now the sexes are mixed and people come and go, which means that the cafés are becoming social affairs and losing their old flavour.

None of them has changed more than the Gijón in the Recoletes. I have always had an affection for that haunt, even though the waiters are slower and the drinks dearer than in most places I know. Through all its phases it has managed to keep its indefinably bogus air. The tables have black and white marble tops like a Victorian wash-stand, pillars break up one's view of the room, there are bracketed lamps on the wall and behind the bar is a long arty mural depicting dice, bottles, playing cards, brushes and palettes and guitars. Bulls for once do not figure. The melancholy story of the Gijón is a little like that of the Café Royal in London. Only a few years ago it was full of shaggy men and dishevelled women in various forms of fancy dress, poring over manuscripts or displaying canvases or wrangling about life as they waved their cigarettes. I used to eye them respectfully but with suspicion, for any Spanish writer or artist I ever knew was fully occupied twenty hours out of the twenty-four in keeping body and soul together. The fame of the Gijón spread, and soon half the clientele were bourgeois like me, eyeing the other half with respectful suspicion. Then the fame spread wider yet, until it became entirely full of bourgeois, eyeing each other in the disrespectful certainty that this is not at all what they came to see. And at the moment of writing it is closed for *obras*.

Once or twice I have been invited to a *tertulia* there, and deplorable affairs they were. They usually started well, with black coffee and epigrams and existentialism, but soon tailed off in gossip and Fundador. This may have been the fault of us women: men have told me that all-male *tertulias* are quite different, the literary artistic and philosophical questions of the day then being thrashed out in a style profound and brilliant at once. Triviality is excluded: the whole affair is a long intellectual feast. But how is a poor woman to discover if this be true? we seem to have heard the tale before. For my part, I strongly doubt it. Abstract ideas are alien to the Spanish mind, which perhaps is one reason why their poets are so good.

Intellectuals gathered too in the dim recesses of the Cocodrilo, but they were mostly of another kind. The wild men at the Gijón were of the tribe that can never do with the world at all and love to flaunt their difference and display their contempt. Those of the Cocodrilo were men of intellect and goodwill, frustrated not only by the present form of their society but by certain fixed qualities in their own people. The lack of ordinary culture among even intelligent Spaniards is staggering: there is no need to ask them if they have read any good books lately for it may be assumed they have read none at all. They have little idea of what a book is, still less what goes to the making of it. An English writer tells the story of a Spanish visitor staring round his library with its hundreds of volumes and exclaiming in wonder "And you wrote all these!" There are educated Spaniards who have never read Don Quixote: many could not name one title of Pérez Galdós or Unamuno. Indifference to books naturally means acquiescence in censorship, and to the intellectuals with their European ideas and liberal theories the fantastic mediaeval censors of Spain are a thorn in the flesh.

An air of quiet desperation, then, hung about the assemblies at the Cocodrilo; and, to be candid, the discussions were of no very great interest, being entirely predictable. Revolt imposes a conformism of its own, and to be anti-Church, anti-Government, anti-bourgeois and anti-tradition was de rigueur. No one of the enemy camp could ever be allowed credit for anything. And there is a suppleness in this stiff-necked race that is baffling to people of happier lands. Someone will fulminate against the censorship, on and on and on until you wonder how he knows so much about it; and then it turns out that he is himself a censor. A journalist excuses himself for writing the contrary of what he thinks on the grounds that the editor ordered it. And these time-servers are quite unabashed. A man with a job feels justified in doing anything to keep it and integrity is a luxury that goes with wealth.

Nothing would ever get me to a tertulia to-day. Talking by the hour in a smoky café is for people young enough to feel that time is unending. For those young enough too, in Madrid, there was the spice of danger. We felt brave and formidable and we half expected to be carried off to the *Seguridad* in the Puerta del Sol to rot there with, it was estimated by us, twenty thousand others. Our peril seemed all the greater because the Spanish members of the company would never lower their voices. Spaniards seldom do, either because such a thing does not come naturally to this noble race or because they are unable. They would bark away at the top of their lungs about the monstrous ban on free speech while the rest of us anxiously wondered if the little man at the table behind were "all right". A man in plain clothes did once come up and flash a police card at one of our number, asking him to go outside. Our hearts flew into our mouths but it was merely to say a flower-pot had fallen from a window on to his father-in-law's head, and would he please go home. Truly is it said, the wicked flee when none pursueth.

Delectable as it once was I now leave it all to others, along with political passion and interior monologue. The way to enjoy a café is to sit there in peace with the brain hardly working at all. Sooner or later the barrier of men outside will shift and before a new one replaces it there may be time for a look at the crowds, hurrying or strolling past according to the time of day. Such problems as occur to the mind do not overtax it. How can prawns be so fresh, so far from the sea? Why does the waiter pour the beer from such a height? Why will Spanish women dye their hair? The newspaper is a source of unending interest. A bus has fallen over the cliff on the way up to Ronda: this need surprise no one. A criminal has been sentenced to thirty years' hard labour and a fine of Pesetas 65 : that fine must have been the last straw. Strings of people have died, to the grief of countless relations. A doctor asks for space in which to declare that the motoring accident he was newly involved in was, in his view, the fault of the other party. Spain has now perfected the form of government suited to the world of to-day and "continues to be the light of West and East alike". Captivating little scenes are going on the whole time. A shoeblack surreptitiously wrenches the heels off a foreign client's shoes and tacks some new ones on: there is going to be a shindy in a minute when he claims a fee for his nefarious act. A nun, her face hidden in the white wings of her cap, goes from table to table begging for an orphanage. She tows a grizzling orphan along by the hand because "charity" and "orphanage" are but colourless abstractions and Spaniards will take it all in better with the peevish little lump right there before their eyes. A gipsy with her hair in a raven plait down her back waves lottery tickets and shouts abuse if they are not bought. And all round are voices, voices, voices, from the peahen cry of the mating female to the gasping wheeze of old gentlemen whose vocal chords have thrown up the sponge for good: voices of every conceivable pitch and timbre, with just one thing in common, that seemingly they never tire. What can there be in this our earthly span to give rise to such an inexhaustible flow? The minutes are slipping past but we plead with ourselves for just a little while longer. And more minutes slip past and we cannot decide to go quite yet. It is so pleasant here, this truly is the clean well-lighted place, and the dusk is turning blue and to westward the sky has that apricot blush of evening skies in Madrid. No one else is in a hurry, why should we be? we are as well placed here as anywhere in the world.

❧ *II* ❧

THE DAY IN MADRID IS FULL AND SEEMINGLY WITHOUT
end, like the days of childhood. Late luncheon cuts into the
afternoon, the weakest part of any day, and dinner at eleven
brings fresh vigour and appetite for life just as Europe in
general is beginning to doze. Time in France and England
is parcelled out like the land, an affair of neat little spaces and
walls in good condition: in Spain it sprawls nonchalantly
ahead as far as the eye can see. In the early part of 1961 it was
decreed that this should change and the clock-habits of the
outer world be introduced: why, only Heaven can say. The
news vexed and troubled foreigners who enjoyed the *madrileño*
way of life and themselves came from democratic countries.
Reared in servile obedience to the law at home, and dupes of
their own propaganda, they believed that conditions here
would be the same or worse. How grievously they had
wronged, how foolishly under-estimated, the inhabitants of
the capital was not slow in becoming clear. Or, it may be, there
was something in the very essence of Spanish time that did not
lend itself to regulation; or again, something deep down in the
regulator himself that was aware of this fact and perfectly
resigned to it. In the famous, and inevitable, phrase, *se obedece
pero nò se cumple*. Apart from freaks who genuinely approve
the cafeteria system and of choice adopt the snack-bar way of
life, the people suit themselves.

This is a fact of Spanish existence that may usefully be borne
in mind. Laws in the democratic lands find their mark, winging
their way to it as surely as arrows into the body of St Sebastian.
In Spain they are shot into the air and fall to ground, we know

not where. Less than a year after the long luncheon break and *siesta* had been "abolished" it was frankly conceded that on the whole the plan was a failure. At the same time, however, it was spiritedly decreed that night life in Madrid should be at an end by half-past one in the morning. At this hour people normally would be leaving their places of entertainment and thinking of paying a visit to the café, looking as fresh as if they had just got out of bed. The sparkle and glitter and animation of the streets persisted to three and four and occasional early risers would see people wearing their evening clothes in broad daylight. There is something agreeably raffish about it, and it would be sad if Madrid were to take on the detrimental habits of the bourgeois north. It is true that for some time now the trend in various provincial towns has been towards less going out and earlier closing down, but it has occurred naturally and spontaneously: a decree is always, in that delightful and expressive word, *contraproducente*, so that there is still hope.

I have often wondered if this very unlikelihood of their being obeyed is why Spanish decrees are often so strange. It seems as if someone were indulging in a form of lunatic self-expression, secure in the knowledge that no harm, or indeed anything else, will result. To give an example, there were two famous ones that in their joyous, antic dissociation from all known laws of economy seemed to verge on the surrealist. First, in order to make the workers happy a general rise of forty per cent. in pay was ordered, regardless of the ability or worth of the individual, the means of the employer or the state of the business. Prices immediately flew up, and then came the second brilliant notion; it was decreed that they were to return to their previous level at once, and remain there. Now every shop window sported a placard to say that in this particular establishment they were unchanged, while they continued their upward flight from week to week in full view of Party, police and public.

In this happy spiritual climate there gradually bubbles up in us a feeling of personal liberty that is all the headier and more delicious for being a surprise. We are so much in the habit of congratulating ourselves on our freedom that we grow blind to the nets that are woven about us. I once read out to some Spanish friends a leaflet from the English Ministry of Agriculture, issued while postwar rationing was in force and laying down the conditions under which a free-born Briton was allowed to keep a pig. There were four pages of regulations, and the smiles grew broader as the reading went on. When it came to where the pig-keeper was to feed the pig himself and not to pay or delegate anyone else to do so, and that by "feed" the Ministry of Agriculture meant "serving with food at meal-times", the audience collapsed altogether. Their laughter was a tribute to the leaflet as a piece of imaginative writing, however: they had no idea, and it was hard to make them believe, that these preposterous rules had ever been obeyed, on the whole freely and willingly, and – it was humiliating to admit – without the coercion of secret or armed police.

"You must stay here with us," they said kindly, patting my arm.

The strong wine of freedom may turn the foreigner's head and lead him astray. Seeing the law disregarded on all sides, in great matters and small, he will conclude that it may safely be left out of accounting altogether, with grave hazard to himself. And when the law is, suddenly and swiftly and implacably, brought home it is likely to be because there has been breach of custom too, and custom is never to be taken lightly. There was at one time a misguided foreigner in the south who indulged in all manner of wild parties and fanciful carryings-on, yet was foolish enough not to make the proper gentleman's agreement with the local police; a false economy if ever there was one, for presently he found himself in gaol on charges carrying a penalty of up to forty years.

That, however, is some little distance away from the subject of time in Madrid. We may sit over our breakfast of cool coffee with sugary buns and apricot jam or, if we like it better, with garlic toast and olive oil, and peacefully think how to spend it. There is no need to plan the day before or make uncomfortable early starts or carry baskets of food with us, for there is time and to spare for everything and meals are there whenever we happen to want them. We can go as far as Aranjuez or the Escorial or even Toledo and still be back to dine before the theatre; and in June it is well worth going to Aranjuez and back for the asparagus alone, the superb white asparagus that must be about the best in the world. Brought up in the superstition that taste and size are incompatible, that asparagus ought to be green with purple tips and can only thrive in a moist climate near the sea, for a long while I would not touch it: thus humanity fights its own happiness. To this day the fat white stalks, gritty with the hot dry yellow soil in which they grew, are a perpetual reminder of the evils of ignorance and prejudice.

In June, moreover, there are two other delightful things, which are strawberries and water. The weeping willows trail their arms in the dimpled surface of the river and the pools in the formal gardens are full to the brim: the parks in the summer palaces are shady and green while the countryside around them bakes and bleaches in the sun. Green is much in our minds as we drive from Madrid under a sky pale with heat and through the rolling arid orange slopes: one grows hungry for green in the Castilian summer. We may leave the Palace and the Casa del Labrador and Godoy's little château on the river bank to the tourists: the rooms are so rich and fussy and ornate as to make one hot merely by looking at them. I never can see those opulent apartments without thinking of Lope de Vega's house in the Calle de Cervantes, with its bare frugal rooms, its plain wood, leather, iron and earthenware, and with the stone well in the garden, the doves on the tree, all in the best tradition of Castilian sobriety. But Lope de Vega kept his furniture in his skull, and had no need of externals to tell him who he was. It must have been both fatiguing and bewildering to live between those embroidered-silk walls, under those painted ceilings, surrounded by those crowds of priceless *objets d'art*; and perhaps a little of the Bourbon giddiness may be put down to the dazing effect of the environment.

Outside is the place to be, then, under the great trees that make a ceiling of foliage not only denser than do the same species when grown in the north, but also much higher. In parts we may walk, as in a tropical forest, in a mysterious cool green twilight, aware that somewhere far above the sun is vainly trying to bake us up. The gardens are planted with roses and jasmine and different fragrant flowering shrubs, birds sing on the boughs and water gurgles from the gardener's hose and in the irrigation ditches. Thereby is exploded another old myth, namely that watering plants in hot sun causes them to wither and droop. On either side of the bridge in the town is a good restaurant and we may lunch at the water's edge there, listening to its pleasant lap-lap-lap and idly watching the launches chugging up and down, weighed down to the very surface by a huge load of cheerful shouting Spaniards, not one of whom, at a guess, would be able to swim but who wriggle and leap and change their places as if the fate of their vessel left them unmoved.

Later, as the evening draws on, we can tour the numbers of little booths at the roadside with their stout bundles of asparagus and boxes of clear red juicy strawberries. Not by any means should we take the first that offer, because asparagus and strawberries are highly important matters, and when we lay them before our friends in Madrid the question of size, flavour, condition and price will be gone into thoroughly. So we will go from one stall to another, laughing and chatting with the vendors and very likely ending up with a peasant's straw hat or a bird in a cage as well. Then we must go. One of these days we are going to spend a night in Aranjuez in order to see the moon shining on the waters, to hear the nightingales and to catch delectable whiffs from the night-scented shrubs in the royal garden. Everyone should have a store of such little dreams for "one of these days" but now, before the strawberries collapse, we will hurry back refreshed in body and rejoiced at heart to the scalding pavements of Madrid.

We can do all that. We can equally well sit and think how nice it would be to do it, and then decide to do something else. We can send for more coffee, saying how glad we should be if it could be really hot and strong this time, and drink the cool fawn-coloured liquid at our leisure when it comes. There is no hurry.

Hours may be profitably spent wandering about the Retiro, one of the finest parks in Europe with its mingling of formality and rustic freedom, its finely laid borders and carefully placed statues and the strange little boskies here and there. There is always something to watch in the Retiro, from the unfortunate people trying to learn to drive under a hail of witticisms from their fellow citizens to the boatmen ramming or capsizing each other on the lake or the dwarf in ragged shirt and trousers who sells rubber toys near one of the gates. The dolls make grotesque faces when their heads are pulled out or pushed in and the little creature tries to make them funnier still by exploiting his own deformity. He shambles to and fro on the outsides of his feet like an ape, he makes faces more awful than the dolls themselves, he cracks jokes in a falsetto voice with his pumpkin head laid coyly on one shoulder. A perpetual crowd of people stand round him and look on, entranced as always by misfortune, but nobody buys a doll. I saw the dwarf in desperation once single a man out, squealing at him for God's sake to buy one, he is hungry, he wants to eat. The man shook his head, laughing, and fumbled in his pocket for a coin: whereat the dwarf held up a tiny hand and, in a man's voice, quietly said, "*Gracias, no.*" The impact of the two words was tremendous, like a rock flung into water and ringing and rippling the surface long after it has sunk to the ground. In Spain such things are always in wait round some corner: I still can see the look in the manikin's eyes as he spoke, the same eloquent tormented eyes as look out of the Velázquez canvases too, and the man's careless shrug and behind them the boys shouting and splashing on the lake, the boatman calling in vain that their hour was up.

The morning is so long that it is possible to drop into a hairdresser without an appointment and still have time left for a more serious activity before luncheon. Not that a visit to a *peluquería* is un-serious, far from it, it can even be terrifying. It is a jungle air we breathe there among the rows of women having their tresses dyed in every shade of war-paint from magenta to honey, while their talons drip scarlet, their voices effortlessly surmount the shindy of the driers and they stare at themselves in the mirrors with the fixed, intense and humourless gaze of Latin women undergoing embellishment. Pleasanter and more reassuring are the masculine haunts of the *limpiabotas*, but the sojourn in them is all too short: one would have to be four-footed to get a chance of savouring it.

One of my very first impressions of Spain years and years ago was the contrast of brilliant shoes and stubbly chins on the men. With us a man would shave every day if it were the last thing he did, and perhaps not be too perturbed if his shoes were a little dusty or dull, while the Spaniard will have his shoes cleaned twice or even three times in a day if he thinks it called for and, to judge from the looks of some, will visit the barber but once or twice a week. And sometimes, glancing through a barber's window and noting his victim pinioned there, head thrown back, nose held in iron grip and a sinister long-handled razor blade such as Sweeney Todd would revel in hungrily licking his throat, I have understood this. The fetish of the clean shoe is supposed to be a survival from the days when the Spanish gentleman did no work and rode everywhere on a horse. Plebeians hoped by wearing clean shoes to be taken for *caballeros* much as when Miss Nancy Mitford issued her famous bull on U and Non-U in English usage a multitude of honest folk mugged up the former in the belief that they were acquiring status. The theory strikes me as far-fetched because Spaniards live in too rigid a society to go in for pretence of that kind. In the fluid condition of a country like England, where whole classes as well as individuals are always coming up, hence treading on the heels of their former "betters" and demanding recognition from them, there is no end to all the nonsense. Unless he is very brilliant or very lucky, however, a Spaniard is apt to stay where he is born, so that he neither runs after the Joneses nor struggles to keep up with them; further, he has a profound conviction of the fundamental equality before God of all men, or anyhow of all Spaniards, and a very lively notion of his own particular excellence. He would not try to look like a *caballero*, for he assumes that he is one. The glittering shoe is more likely to be a sign of his estimable dandyism: whatever his rank a Spaniard will try to look as well dressed as he can – in civilian clothes, that is to say: uniform is another matter – and even a poor man can usually afford a shoeblack. The stubble on his chin is another question and does not worry him at all, indeed he probably values it as a manifestation of virility. But whatever the underlying cause, the institution of the *limpiabotas* is admirable and delightful, whether it is of the ambulatory kind that snuggles up to you in the café or that which operates in dim parlours with marble floors, mysteriously associated with stamps, cigarettes and lottery tickets, just as in France *vin ordinaire* mysteriously goes with olive oil, logs and charcoal.

On visiting Madrid last I had the horrible experience of finding that "my" *limpiabotas* had been swept away. Knowing foreigners are rather apt to have "their" *bistrot*, restaurant, barber and so on and to claim that these are in some way special and better than others. They drag their friends off to eat stewed cat in a den at Levallois or a *pizza* like plaster of Paris in

Trastevere, assuring them with honest pride that they discovered the place for themselves and begging them not to tell anyone else. Nevertheless, it does seem to me that "my" *limpiabotas* was remarkable in every way. To begin with it was beautifully placed, beside "my" hotel in the Alcalá and a few steps from the Puerta del Sol. It was only a short distance further to the cafés Lion d'Or or La Tropical, so that I arrived for breakfast in the high morale that goes with dazzling shoes. In the opposite direction, round the Sol, lay the captivating old streets and the Plaza Mayor, the rich racy eighteenth-century Madrid of which one never grows tired. Off the Sol was the Calle de la Victoria, which equally well might be called The Street of the Wonderful Faces, where tickets for the *corridas* are sold at official prices in official *taquillas*, and hence there is always a shouting jostling mob of blackmarketeers outside them, swearing to heaven that the very last ticket for Thursday or Sunday has gone; and yet that they may be able to get some for you, through influence and with great trouble to themselves, and at a commensurate price. Up a little further again, beyond Jerónimo and also to the right, there is Echegaray. Three pesetas will buy you here a glass of delicious wine in an old dark tavern, fragrant with bunches of dried herbs and aromatic roots suspended from heavy wooden beams across the ceilings and hung about with ancient *típico* pictures and engravings. At some of the little restaurants up and down you get some of the best cooking in Madrid at remarkably low rates. There are the *tascas* as well, with their portly wine barrels and their assortment of snacks, *angulas*, the tiny wormy eels from the Bay of Biscay that are fried in a rich mess of oil, garlic and chili, the prawns, octopi and squids, alarming to see but delicious to eat, and miraculously fresh, as well as the mushrooms, fried peppers, spiced sausages and, special to Madrid, the tripe. Not all the eating houses are good, and experience can be a brutal teacher. Establishments paved in coloured tiles depicting the Three Graces or a Spanish

138

general drawing his sword in defence of civilization should be avoided always: the food will be cooked in crude olive oil and ten to one there will be a juke-box. In this fascinating quarter one could moon the morning away all too easily and return at leisure to the *limpiabotas* to be shined up again at the end of it.

But its position was by no means its only charm. The bootblacks, young and old, were all masters of their profession and men of cultivated and distinguished minds. Many of them had blue eyes, and for some mysterious reason blue eyes in a Spaniard are a good sign. When an old customer dropped in after a long absence their greeting was laconic rather than effusive, but they knew just how long it was since he last was there, and they remembered where he usually stayed or ate and what he liked to see in the theatre. If a customer wanted an errand run one of the brotherhood emitted a piercing whistle and a youth of amiable but sluggish disposition came slouching in to take the order. To make people feel thoroughly at home and soothed and contented in the brief space of time they spent there was an achievement requiring ages of civilization behind it.

There was atmosphere in that parlour too, by which I mean that particular feel about a particular place which in Spain is usually communicated by human beings and not by places at all. It is perhaps a question of water: those subtle emanations cannot survive in this sharp dry air which conserves the material casing but drives the spirits out. Galicia is the exception, rainy Galicia of the trailing mist and dewy cobweb and blurred horizon, of the ghosts and witches and the sidelong glances. In the moist air of the north things crumble and moulder and if some intangible presence did not linger about their remains there would be little to speak of the past to us. Here is no need to evoke the past for it lies spread out before our eyes. The magic air of Spain preserves equally modes of life or brick and stone, so that the past becomes a matter of simple continuity, nostalgia-free. The peculiar sensation that a great historical English house or a ruined castle in Ireland or an ancient temple of Japan may give us will very likely arise here from some everyday activity of ordinary people. Some of us once made a kind of pilgrimage to the birthplace of the Archpriest of Hita, in Alcalá de Henares near Madrid. I suppose we had heard him called the Spanish Chaucer so often that we half expected to catch echoes like those that even to-day sound faintly here and there along the pilgrim's road to Canterbury; but there was nothing, nothing but scorched treeless land and blank baking stone. We knew the wayward genius first saw light in this region but he did not hang about it as Shakespeare hangs round Stratford.

A few days after that excursion I happened to go to the sacristy of the local parish church to fetch a *bula*, the permission to eat meat on Friday which is available to all Spaniards as a reward for expelling the Moors and which they generously extend, for a small fee, to those who can claim no part in that operation. And there suddenly, somehow, before me in the dingy office was everything there had not been in Alcalá de Henares. Nothing much happened. Seven or eight priests, some smoking cigars, some with their hats on their heads, most of them requiring a shave, all with good round bellies and in high good humour, were sitting at a long table. In the middle of it stood a vast washerwoman's hamper full to the brim with soiled paper money, and this they contemplated with lively satisfaction. They smiled jovially on hearing my errand and bade me return on the morrow: addressing me, however, as "chica", which at my time of life is so pleasant as to rob inconvenience of any sting. A slice of the Archpriest's world, the merry and accommodating clerical world of the fourteenth century, was there, alive and kicking. It was an odd, delightful experience such as frequently comes in Spain, in places like the one described, or in the arena or the market-place: and in the boot-blacking parlour of fond memory in the

Alcalá. I used to hurry there each morning with the same pleasurable anticipation as to a theatre. And then it was all gone one day, and in its place, horrible to say, stood a milk-bar: empty, thank God, but a milk-bar for all that, with bottles of the stuff lined up in a pallid vacant hygienic grin and a pert señorita where once grave shoeblacks worked and throve. *Ahime! Eheu! Nous n'irons plus aux bois, les lauriers sont coupés....*

THE FINEST COLLECTION OF PAINTINGS IN EUROPE IS
housed in a pink and fawn-coloured building set among grassy
banks and green trees, with the spires of San Jerónimo el Real
rising above it in the background. The exterior of the Prado
is simple, homely and faintly comic. Its façade is enlivened
by a row of plump ladies in grimy stone, denoting
Magnificence, Fertility, Admiration, Power, Fame and other
such symbols of euphoria. Inside, time goes at a pace of its
own as if dissociating itself from time in the rest of the capital.
The doors seem barely to have opened when the attendants
begin to rattle their keys and drape the postcard stands with
their own peculiar glee. That is to say, those attendants who
are in the great old tradition and either ignore visitors until
the moment they can be turned out or treat them as potential
felons. A truly dedicated follower of this tradition, standing
within a few yards of the Lady of Elche, will have it that no
such work has ever existed. It all goes together with bristly
chins and garlicky breath and ankle-length overcoats and, like
many ancient institutions to-day, is threatened by newly
emerging forces. A race is springing up who not only know
what their Museum contains and where to find it but are willing
and even eager to share their knowledge.

For years I have been intending to work methodically
through the collection, but invariably stick in the Spanish
rooms. These become ever more absorbing with familiarity,
for every Spanish quality is here in one form or another, the
extravagance, the earthiness, the harshness, the illusion and

disillusion, the gay and grotesque, the humming *muchadumbre* of bees in the Spanish bonnet. The themes are God and Man, nature getting a bare look in. Landscape is used as a setting only, usually in the form of a park or a purely conventional line of hills or trees. Even as rural a picture as "Los Borrachos" was painted in Velázquez' studio and the low foothills of the Guadarramas put in from memory. Perhaps the very grandeur of the country itself has something to do with it, perhaps the material is too intractable, too wild and stubborn and on too vast a scale to compose, glaring under too harsh a light. Whatever the reason, a Spanish Constable or Monet or Van Gogh is somehow unthinkable.

The religious painting faithfully expresses the national temperament, that is to say, it is inspired more easily by the Crucifixion, the Virgin weeping below the Cross, the martyrdoms of saints and apostles, by bones, skulls, flagellations and the torments of hell than by the Joyful Mysteries. Good Friday rather than Easter is the day for the Christians of Spain. What a feeling of personal grief there is at the hour of Christ's death! Not only in the churches where among the swathed images, empty fonts and extinguished lamps crowds kneel in adoration of the Host which, enthroned in a bank of flowers and candles, is the one sign of hope left in an almost brutal desolation, but in the streets and houses as well. Flags fly at half-mast, people go in mourning, voices are kept low, even to chuckle in a public place is to invite reproachful looks. It is as if all these stoic pent-up men and women had saved their private tears to add them once in the year to a universal flood. Easter is a different story, it is something of an anticlimax, there is the Easter duty to perform, processions to watch, then probably a family luncheon, a *corrida* in the afternoon and fireworks at night. It is *fiesta*, even *gran fiesta*, but it does not move the people in the way that Good Friday does, nor is there the burst of joy in the air that is felt on Easter Day in Greek or Russian orthodox churches.

So then it is the human side rather than the divine of Christ's nature and life that the Spanish painter is drawn to and those artists who excel in the human sphere appear to me to do so in the religious. It may be a quirk of taste but the religious work of Velázquez and Zurbarán, even of Goya, move me more than that of El Greco or Murillo, perhaps by their down-to-earth quality. If we go right up to "La Adoración de los Reyes" we see a Virgin with a dull peasant face holding a Child who looks all too sharp and knowing, a future *cacique* you might think, while He receives the homage of three clodhoppers. If we stand a little way off, the picture exudes reverence, tranquillity and love, all through a simple but magic use of light and shade. Beside the matter-of-fact presentations of Velázquez the "spirituality" of an El Greco subject with the anaemic face, the upturned eyes and the spiky mole's hands seems trite.

To the portrayal of human beings the great Spanish artists bring all the raciness and observation and irony that pervade Spanish literature. Truth comes first, without regard to power or place, let alone to compassion or chivalry. What court painter but a Spanish one would risk showing his king as a red-faced bumpkin and his queen as the very pattern of misguided vanity, with lasciviously sparkling button eyes, a flat nose and thin lips compressed to hide the missing teeth? Such indeed were that catastrophic pair, Carlos IV and Maria Luisa, by all contemporary accounts and it seems not to have occurred to Goya to depict them in any other way. Nor, for that matter, do we hear that they were anything but delighted with his performance.

There is the portrait by Velázquez of the Infanta Margarita, small hands firm on the huge frothing and shimmering skirt of red and silver, the curls shining, the wide confident eyes incuriously fixed on their great delineator, the Hapsburg cheek bulging a little as if over a lollipop, the Hapsburg nose already bulbing, the Hapsburg arrogance none too far away, all in a marvellously suspended animation. The Mother Jerónima de la Fuente, grasping her crucifix as other women grasp an axe, reminds us of every shrewd hard patient old Spanish nun we have ever seen. When Velázquez painted her she was waiting in Seville to take ship for Manila to found the convent of Santa Clara there; but we may still run across her at any time, marshalling her orphans along a dusty road, resolutely extracting alms from people in cafés, totting up the accounts of her convent, telling her beads in a come-no-nonsense manner on the wooden seat of a crowded and appalling train, a creature not of to-day, to-morrow or yesterday but of always, a drab brown figure expressive not only of the woman but of her land and her Church, painted when Velázquez was twenty-one.

The famous dwarfs, or *bufones*, stand in a row, Don Diego de Acedo, a Court official and not a jester at all, who set up to be the painter's cousin and a man of letters, a tiny creature in black with a hat far too big and cocked at an angle of defiance who holds a book half the size of his body and who is fairly swelling with a secret importance, all against a background of wintry chaos: Don Sebastian de Morra, jester to the Prince Cardinal in the Low Countries, who fancied himself as traveller and man of the world: the idiot boy from Vallecas, Lezcano, said to have been born with all his teeth, here vacantly staring and holding some cards in his feeble little hands, used as the butt and recreation of young Prince Baltasar Carlos; and then Calabacillas, or Little Pumpkins, of imbecile appearance but with a turn of wit that Philip IV relished. All of them in the nakedness of their despair and of their futile attempts to escape have the power to excite horror and arouse compassion in us centuries after the ending of their short and luckless lives and all may be seen any day in the flesh hawking their lottery tickets in the street or at the church door.

I seldom go through these rooms, where one masterpiece follows the other in a dazzling array, without thinking of the king's obstinate endeavours to make an *hidalgo* of Velázquez. No pains were spared, no euphemisms shirked, points were stretched to the point of bursting: wearisome research went on to prove the painter a man of pure Spanish blood, free from the Jewish or Moorish taint, a descendant of people who never had traded or served, an artist who painted by his sovereign's order or to please himself, and never for vile money. All this was to make him acceptable to the Noble Order of Santiago, for which he was repeatedly proposed by Philip IV and as often rejected by the Order, with an obduracy no less rigid than the king's and which provides a remarkable footnote to Spanish absolutism. One can understand the attitude of the king, for rank seems all-important to those who have it and little beyond, but how to explain that of the artist? To be Velázquez, and to yearn to be "Don Diego"! Behold, what a piece of work is a man.

Now and again when receptivity weakens it is a capital thing to sit down and observe the human scene. Every time I go in I recognize certain individuals of cultured appearance and aspect mild and vague who, I believe, have made the building their permanent home. They have the look of people who never go out and one suspects that were they ever to do so they would be run over almost at once. In here they move purposefully and with assurance from one canvas to the next and their comments, if any, are brief and to the point: they seem unaware rather than scornful of the philistines round them who are commenting in a blithe lowbrow way that Don Carlos is the image of Onkel Ignaz, *nicht*? or that the "Maja Desnuda" will catch her death and serve the hussy right; and they look so hungrily at a painting it seems as if their eyes will draw the colour out.

These are a peculiar species of *fauna*, not painters themselves but experts on the matter of painting. They know everything except how to do it; ask them a question concerning dates, attributions, influences, and they will rap out the answer like a machine telling your weight. Another Prado species worthy of note is the copyist, who provides us with material for long if fruitless speculation. Why has the lady with the bobbed white hair and the blouse of one blue and the skirt of another picked "Los Borrachos" for her model? She inhabits a little world of cheap pensions and valiant doing-without: what has she to do with Velázquez', ribald old topers, with Bacchus of the sly smooth face and vine-wreathed head egging them on, a young Smart Alec making a fool of elders and betters? She screws up her fierce little virgin's face and glares at the glorious sunlit abandon before her, then rapidly puts in a stroke or two of the brush and steps back to admire the effect. Steal a glance at her work and the mystery deepens. Were it not for the plump white torso of Bacchus and the ruby glow on the peasant's features one would hardly guess what it was intended to be.

The young man who copies Goya's "Maja Desnuda" has a more promising air. Someone or other copies it every day but this poor young man has Artist written all over him. He must be a genius, with his wild eyes and hollow cheeks and the little fringe of despondent beard. The cotton trousers are dirty and torn and toes poke out of the rope-soled shoes. It is plain that he denies himself everything to buy paints and brushes and canvas. Now and again he fervently rumples his long black hair. With lively anticipation we peep over his shoulder and *caramba!* what do we see? Goya's exquisite line and delicate luminous flesh has turned into a mauvish lump of meat. But the young man works away with the same forgetfulness of self and dedication as the little old lady in blue, and as the wan individual in the smock and velvet beret who seems to have wandered out of "La Vie de Bohème", and as the scowling fellow with the head and shoulders of a *picador*.

I must describe the harrowing experience of one morning, very early, so early that I had achieved the universal ambition and got "Las Meninas" to myself. There I stood, half expecting

one of the miraculous figures to give a sign of life: Mari-
Bárbola perhaps, who from the look on her broad dwarf's
face seemed on the verge of passing some remark about me,
something sharp and disagreeable and witty, to make the little
Infanta and her ladies burst out laughing: or the mastiff, who
after four centuries might suddenly lose patience and turn to
snap at Nicolasito Pertusato's foot as it dug him in the flank;
or Velázquez himself, who might call out to bystanders to
go away before they spoiled the composition of the group. It is
difficult to contemplate this stupendous picture without bursting into cliché, as we see from the ejaculations of notables
listed in the *catalogue raisonné*, including the "What! are they
still alive?" of that naughty old fraud, the Countess d'Aulnoy,
who never saw it at all. I gazed and gazed, feeling all the satisfaction tinged with melancholy that great art gives and hoping
no one would come just yet, for one could stand there by the
hour and never be tired of it.

At this moment a woman, blonde and stringy and with
bright hypnotic eyes, approached and in germanic accents
revealed that the painting was thought by many to be Velázquez' masterpiece. She gave an account of it and of the
figures included, with dates and biographical matter, and drew
attention to many felicities that without her aid I must undoubtedly have overlooked. She hunted me hither and yon to
study it the better from this angle and that, she explained that
the mirrors were put there because the picture seen thus at one
remove came more magically alive than ever and forced me to
try them and confirm that it was so. This fiend, it is perhaps
worth remarking, looked for no reward: it merely had not
crossed her mind that anyone else could know anything and
she was urged on by an appalling lust for communication.

One swallow does not make a summer and accordingly I
hesitate to classify this scourge among the Prado species: yet
when at last she roamed away in search of fresh woods and
pastures new and the room filled up with a herd of young

ladies from some good convent it struck me that I had undergone that same experience before, in that very same place and with that same terrible lady or one exactly like her. Did then a species exist? or was she but the Phantom of the Prado? I will probably never know, but I can never approach the "Maids of Honour" now without throwing uneasy glances round me.

The human spectacle is one of never failing interest and amusement, with every now and then a little chink appearing in the wall of bodies so that we may catch a glimpse of a painting. There are the great crowds of foreigners, whose faces have turned the colour of boiled shrimps in the sun and seem on the point of expiring with heat. Rich old American ladies in teenager hats seem to preponderate, growling to each other over the souvenir stands in hoarse manly voices: Germans frown at the catalogue as if to warn it they will stand none of its nonsense, French ask the way to the *salas franceses* before anything else, English move briskly as if taking the dog for a walk; and there are Asians, Indians, Africans, people from all over the world who, however, tend in the presence of Art to divide into three main groups, the reverent, the truculent and the facetious. Spaniards are noticeably in a minority and apart from priests, nuns and their little charges very often the only ones in sight are couples on their honeymoon, this being a moment of life when the Spanish are apt to improve their minds once and for all, so that they need never tinker with them again.

I know several educated Madrileños who have never been in the Prado at all. One of these, a woman, is nevertheless very fond of talking about it and whenever we meet she buttonholes me for news of Goya, Velázquez, Murillo and the other great ones. I must describe it all to her, room by room, as to one without the gift of sight or movement. She is particularly interested in the two singular paintings by Carreño, "La Monstrua Desnuda" and "La Monstrua Vestida", which show a little girl of repulsive fatness, like some little American darling bloated with ice-cream, pie and love, first naked and then richly clothed. We discuss them interminably, speculating as to who the original can be and why anyone, whether patron or artist, should have desired to fix her loathsome form in perpetuity.

"I should so like to see them!"

My friend always accompanies these words with a sigh of longing. In a like wistful manner I have heard people along the Demarara coast speak of "the interior", the deep primeval Amazonian forest. For them, however, it would have meant an expedition of days or weeks, with Indians, mosquitos, kibouri, snakes and probably fever. My friend has only to leave her flat, turn to the right and right again and walk straight on until she comes to the Prado doors: seventeen minutes in all, four or five in a taxi.

"If only I could see them!"

She is, of course, an extreme case.

One could really move into the Prado and spend the rest of one's life there. *Hay de todo*, except baths. In a charming open yard with green shrubs a friendly waitress will serve you mysterious snacks, from combinations dishes with potatoes cheeps to spilt banane. Here, too, the human element adds greatly to the pleasure. One noon there was a fat red smiling man from Lancashire, his shirt open to reveal a furry chest and tummy, sipping a glass of champagne while the bottle lolled in the cooler beside it. No doubt the honest fellow was celebrating his first encounter with the world of art, and I was much edified to think of the opportunities for mental enrichment that the affluent society offers to all. But when I returned to the *cantina* just before it closed there he still was, a little rosier, smiling more widely, high living and low thinking, with various dead bottles lying round him, a curious phenomenon indeed in that frugal ambience. The waitress looked on him with indulgence, as if to say that if he wanted to do his drinking there, so he might. And when you came down to it, he was but killing two birds with one stone, for no one could ever say he had not been to the Prado. I suspect, too, that he was the only man in the room or even the building that Velázquez or Goya would have considered worth painting.

There is seldom a dull moment in the Prado.

❧ *13* ❧

PASTRANA IS TYPICAL OF THE SPAIN THAT WILL LEAVE
incomparable manuscripts to be eaten by mice or wedge a
Zurbarán across a broken window. Compact, perfect, warmly
coloured, it hugs the side of a hill with an air of being the fruit
of a single happy inspiration, somewhat like Ragusa or Venice.
The ducal palace and the collegiate Church of Our Lady of the
Assumption dominate, or rather preside over, a unity of colour,
form and sentiment. A long history and the beauty that has
survived wealth and glory entitle Pastrana to the rank of
ciudad, although nowadays under three thousand people live
in it. It can be reached in a couple of hours from Madrid, the
way passing by Alcalá de Henares, another fallen star, whose
university once rivalled that of Salamanca and now accom-
modates *falangista* officials undergoing a political wash-and-
brush-up: then by Guadalajara, steadily dwindling as well,
having never recovered heart from the ravages of the Civil
War: past Hueva of the leaning church-tower and the cave-
dwellings and through beautiful fertile countryside to the
mediaeval Pastrana itself.

Four of us set out to visit it on a wild wet day soon after
Easter. We had been in two minds as to whether the expedition
should not be called off, in view of the rain implacably falling
in Madrid; but when we got to our destination the rain had
stopped and the tiled roofs of the city seemed to glow more
richly, the new green of silver birch and poplar to look more
intense and the waters of the Arlés more opulent in the soft
hazy air than they might under hard sun. Rosemary, broom,

grape hyacinth and wild orchids were flowering profusely in the rocky scrubby earth on either side of the road and the red-trousered partridge of Spain, the hoopoe and other handsome or unusual birds continually started up as we dashed by.

We stopped in the Plaza de la Hora, in front of the ducal palace whose empty windows stared blankly before them like the eyeholes of a skull. The *plaza* had only two other sides, the fourth being open to a broad view of the river plain with its small terraced patches of cultivation and its round floors for threshing grain. Within the palace courtyard was a scene as *típico* and *auténtico* as the heart could desire. Cocks and hens ran fussily in and out of the great halls of the ground floor, through open doorways we got glimpses of line upon line of washing hung out to dry in the ducal apartments and the court-yard itself had been transformed into an open-air cinema, with electric cables drooping over our heads in an unpretentious but menacing kind of way.

A man came out of his carpentering shed, also within the palace, and conducted us round the building. We particularly wished to see the quarter in which the Princess Eboli, duchess of Pastrana, was kept after her fall and where she presently died. The beautiful but one-eyed lady, a power at the Court of the Emperor Charles V and afterwards a favourite with his son Philip II, spent her last years agonizing in a smallish room with a stone floor and carved wooden ceiling, gazing through an iron grille at such life as went on in the little *plaza* below: until, by order of the same mixed-up monarch whom formerly she had captivated, a sheet of metal was fixed over the window to cut her off entirely. The townspeople nicknamed the wretched captive *La Puta,* the whore. Even Cela accepts that view and, in his delightful notebook on the Alcarria, remarks that the Castilian village is institutional and sacramental and never forgives the rich and great for breaking the commandments of God. But the truth – unromantic as truth is apt to be – is that the Castilian village never forgives the rich and great for being great and rich, and that the stories of La Eboli's licentious conduct in the furtherance of her political schemes are moonshine, figments of the popular mind. Spanish envy is a greater force than even Spanish virtue.

A dismal picture of ruin met our eyes at every turn in this ancient house. The only creatures who seemed comfortable and at home were the barnyard fowl and a swallow or two who had built nests in the beams of the roof. The superbly carved ceilings of hard brown pinewood were turning white or coming away from the walls and roof with damp. Great gaps appeared in them as well, for during the Civil War the place had been occupied by Moorish troops who had prised out section after section of the carvings whenever they were short of firewood. Drops of water rained down through innumerable cracks and empty tins were dotted about on the floor to catch them. Our guide and his family lived in princely discomfort within the building, the whereabouts of their apartment being indicated by a tin stovepipe stuck at an angle through the ducal wall and steadily puffing out a thick brown smoke. He told us that water used to drip on his bed and that he had repaired the roof himself to stop it, but that to do as much for the whole palace was beyond him. This guide was a dark sallow little man with a dry turn of phrase and a sardonic light in his eye which was switched on immediately anyone mentioned dukes, Moors, La Eboli, Jesuits or the Lord Bishop himself.

There the old house stands, with the frame intact, the marble fireplaces unharmed, the *azulejos* or ornamental tilework still beautiful and the façade crumbling but far from destroyed. It is not clear whether the disposing of it lies with the Counts Romanones, the great local family, or with the Society of Jesus; but without enormous expense or preposterous effort it could be restored and used as a museum for the city and the region. More likely it will moulder away year by year, like so much else in Spain, as if the well of the *patrimonio* could never run dry. Cela says, "Pastrana without watchmen or martial airs or the warrior spirit or the Middle Ages is a city like other cities, even though beautiful as few of them are, which rise and fall, flourish or fade, according as the fates are kind or turn them the cold shoulder. In Pastrana perhaps we find a key to something that happens in Spain more often than it ought. Past splendour weighs upon and may even dry up the will-power; and without will, as we can see, the endless contemplation of vanished greatness means a neglect of the problems of the hour. With the belly empty and the head full of golden memories, these memories grow always fainter until in the end, without anyone admitting it, there may even arise some doubt as to whether they were ever true. . . ." The fact is that Spaniards will bother about some things and not about others. From the ducal windows could be seen, perched on the highest point of the city, a little hermit's cell with a *calvario* beside it. On Good Friday, only a few days before, the men of Pastrana had toiled all the way up to it with the heavy *pasos* of the Crucified on their shoulders. The stony narrow track led upward so steeply that the men in front were all but doubled up, while those behind were walking on tiptoe. It probably never even occurred to them that it was rather a lot of trouble.

The *fonda*, where we went for lunch, was housed within the palace too, like the guide's family and workshop, the Servicio Nacional del Trigo, the cocks and hens and swallows and dear only knows what else beside. We went in past a handsome marble pillar by the door with the stoical resolution of people entering a Spanish provincial inn; but it was to meet with a most agreeable surprise. The hostess was a brown smiling middle-aged woman with a profile such as you might see on a Roman coin, who presided over a spotless kitchen and a cooking-stove framed in more rich marble; and she sent up an excellent meal of raw cured ham and spiced sausage, Spanish omelettes, roast *corderito lechal* or sucking-lamb, fruit and sturdy red wine by the jugful. With these good things went one of the most ornamental loaves of bread I have ever seen, beautifully

155

baked with a golden brown crust, looking like the prize entry in a world competition of master bakers. The hostess had lit the stove in the dining-room, using as fuel a loose powdery material that looked like peat moss but was in fact the refuse of olives from which the oil had been pressed out. It burned merrily, quickly warming the whole room. Other people came in, peasants from the country around, commercial travellers or officials, all politely bidding us *aprovechar* as they went by our loaded table.

The inn was named for St Teresa, the saint having founded a convent in the city and spent many a trying moment there. Whether from charity or discretion, in the *Fundaciones* she gives only a very mild account of her vexations, for many of which she could thank La Eboli herself. After the death of her husband the Princess insisted on assuming the habit of the reformed Carmelites and threw herself into a life of humility and privation with all the relish of an arrogant and pampered woman. Indeed, so relentlessly humble and devout was she that St Teresa concluded that it would be better to move the foundation out of her orbit altogether. The operation was planned to take place at dead of night and in great secrecy but needless to say it reached La Eboli's ears; and at the very moment the nuns were preparing to creep away she sent a messenger to say "many things" to them.

When we had finished our meal there was the collegiate church to be seen. The custodian of the palace had promised that a young man who was studying for the priesthood would show us round it; and we found that he had been patiently waiting there ever since he received news of our arrival. He informed us of the fact smilingly but with a faint reproach, as if somehow we ought to have divined his movements. The main treasures here were two fifteenth century tapestries from the famous collection of Alfonso V of Portugal commemorating the capture of Tangier and Arzila by the Portuguese; and very fine they appeared to be although the crypt was too badly lit to allow of their being properly seen. The remainder, despite the pleas of the inhabitants of the city, have been haled off to Madrid in the familiar ruthless way that makes one think of the capital as a vast greedy mouth sucking the country dry. On this subject the normally detached and ironic Cela grows impassioned, crying out that to do this is to kill the provinces off and that it is the provinces, not Madrid, that in effect are the true *pais*. He appeals too for haphazard arrangements, naturalness, spontaneity that will recall the natural order of things and remarks that the cold administrative planning of museums is inhuman and unnatural, which may well be so, although Madrid cannot fairly be reproached with going too far in this direction.

Cela's heart must have leaped up when he beheld the collection of incunabula, although he does not say so. Nothing could have been more natural and haphazard than the way they were lolling about on their stands at the end of the choir, the edges of their dingy vellum leaves all munched away by mice. There is something very attractive in Spanish fecklessness – indeed, in all the Spanish shortcomings – but it is to be feared that a day will come when the last scrap is eaten and these ancient treasures be one more memory. Examining them, we stumbled over a long roll of carpeting dumped on the choir floor and hoped for an instant it might be one of the controversial tapestries; but it proved to be a length of something very up-to-date and hideous, intended for what purpose we could not conceive.

With its large reredos by Juan de Borgoña depicting various saints and martyrs, with its paintings, treasures and chandeliers and the tomb of La Eboli, not to speak of the equipment for a really sumptuous funeral and requiem on which our friend the priestling dwelt with loving pride, the church was well made up for one so out of the way and so little frequented. It also had a wonderful old organ, decorated freely as to its woodwork, the mouths of its pipes round and wide as if massing for an attack on the ears of the faithful: we were only sorry that the sounds it was capable of producing had to be left to our imagination.

When we came into the open air again, it was to make contact with the townspeople. One of our party kept a donkey at home in England and she had let it be known that she would buy a straw pannier for him, if such were to be had. Two or three men were standing near the church door and on the ground between them was a pannier stained with earth and rent with age. Their faces brightened as we came.

"Where is the Señora who wants a pannier? Look! the very thing."

The donkey's mistress examined the object gingerly and asked how much they wanted for it. The actual owner, scratching his armpit, went through the motions of one who with difficulty brings himself to part with an heirloom, who naturally must ask a good price for it and who yet is determined to give the customer a bargain. Other men and boys came drifting up to look on.

"Three hundred pesetas."

We had no idea how much it ought to be but this seemed rather a lot. One of the spectators groaned. In the manner of tourists we stood there helplessly asking each other, "Well, what do you think?"

"Isn't it rather a lot?" we inquired of the owner.

"No," he replied.

What could we do? Besides, we were still on holy ground and did not like to haggle. The deal was concluded. The spectator who had groaned before groaned again, this time putting more of himself into it. Money changed hands, the man of our party took up the pannier and we trudged away, accompanied by the owner, friends and onlookers.

"Now that it is over, please tell me how much it should have been," I muttered to the man who had groaned.

"Fifteen duros!" he said, and spat to one side.

To have paid only four times the proper amount appeared to us a notable achievement and taking leave of our new companions in the Plaza de la Hora with many expressions of mutual esteem we went to celebrate in a little bar across from the ducal palace. And later on, as we strolled through the narrow streets, admiring a fountain, a doorway, an old coat-of-arms, we discovered that we had never been really cheated at all. In a shop that sold wooden farming tools, harness, rosaries, baby's bonnets and boots, hunting-knives, candlesticks and Infants of Prague, we saw a new pannier, fresh and green and almost smelling of the fields, in every way better suited to a Lincolnshire donkey than the grubby torn article in our possession, and immediately we asked the price.

"Three hundred and fifty pesetas."

A mere bagatelle, only fifty more than the other!

"Two hundred and fifty," we bid, no longer being on hallowed ground.

"Pues, cortamos. Tres cientos!"

Thus we got the second for the price of the first and very fair it seemed: and thinking it over we saw that the man who for our sakes had deprived himself and his donkey of the pannier would now have to buy another in its place and, in the light of that, his price too was very fair, indeed dead right. With great satisfaction and the two straw panniers we got into the car and drove away, with the shopkeeper looking after us in mingled amusement and contempt.

Next we went to Zorita de Los Canes and, climbing the hill where stood a ruined castle that once had belonged to the Calatrava Order looked over the prospect below, a wide and fertile plain and the meeting-place of the Tagus and the Arlés, towards the faraway hills. Enormously deep holes, ideal for the placing of awkward persons, yawned in the ground at our feet. Dusk was falling, lights came out one after the other like stars, the dogs were at their evening bark. In the ancient town of Zorita below the people stood by their doorways, chattering.

Many of them were light-eyed and with a reddish tinge in their hair, and of a sturdy build, for once upon a time this had been a Visigothic settlement and the strain had never quite died out.

Stopping only at a wayside inn for a plate of delicious grilled meat and more jugs of good red wine, we drove rapidly back to the evening pleasures of Madrid.

❦ *14* ❦

I SEE A NOTE IN LAST YEAR'S DIARY, "JUNE 16 : TO AVILA by the evening coach". June, Avila, evening, coach: the words suggest horses pulling valiantly stage by stage past rocks and waterfalls along rough mountain tracks until, with a triumphant burst from the horn, they draw up by the Puerta del Alcázar under the phlegmatic eyes of nesting storks. In fact this coach was the familiar diesel-engined monster, crawling with bitter complaints up the horrifying ascent to the Puerto de los Leones de Castilla to an accompaniment of loud thunder and fierce rain. An endless line of other monsters was engaged in the same way, a procession of vast but languid beetles. One of them, hauling a trailer with ten motor-cars on it, five on a top deck and five below, had given up and pulled to the side, unable to go either forward or back. It may well be there to this day. From time to time a flash of lightning lit up the whole magnificent mountain with its dense black pines and huge grey boulders. At the pass itself the thunderstorm abruptly stopped and we slid down the equally horrifying descent in warm sunshine with pink wild roses and yellow broom flowering profusely along the way.

I have seen Avila in all moods and all seasons but that evening the first impression was that everyone had a cold in the head. After the heat and dust of Madrid the air seemed delightfully cool and fresh, but it must have been too much for the inhabitants. As I followed the porter from the station to the hotel every man, woman and child we passed appeared to be coughing, sneezing or blowing a nose. And my clearest memory is of the dinner at the little hotel outside the city wall. For one thing, I encountered the wine of Cebreros, which I never had done before, although I had been through Cebreros itself, a merry little town and somewhat out of place in grave Castile. The waiter had already brought my half-bottle of tourist's *clarete* and was on the point of opening it when my eye fell on a Monseñor at the next table who was pouring wine from an earthenware jug. When clerics of high degree drink at all they often drink what is good, and moreover this worthy man had a little inward smile on his face as he poured that led me to inquire of the waiter what it was. The waiter said it was Cebreros, a regional wine noted for its excellence but unfortunately very strong: he appeared to look on strength in wine as a fault of character. I bade him take his *clarete* back and bring a jug of Cebreros, and a fine stroke of business it turned out to be. The wine deserved all the waiter's praise, the Monseñor's happy smile and more besides. It was in the full sense "generous", rich and warm and gay, the sort of wine that mitigates a poor meal and glorifies a good one. The dinner here was very good indeed, another reason why it lives in my memory, for I had approached it with all the forebodings natural in a veteran traveller.

In spite of its place in the very heart of frugal and sober Castile Avila cooks and eats well. One can have quite a feast off the produce of the region cooked in the regional manner: in fact one of the local brochures suggests a menu for it, which might be a way of passing a wet afternoon. You begin with *níscalos,* small and very delicious mushrooms, fried or grilled, with crabs from the river. Next should come a locally-spiced sausage (*chorizo*) with locally grown red beans (*judías del Barco*). Either trout, carp or red gurnard may supply the fish course; but here I will intervene to say that while Avila trout and carp are as good as can be, red gurnard anywhere is about as vexatious a fish as Europe can provide. It is both spiky and insipid and you may as soon think of eating a woollen sock stuffed with pins. Falstaff evidently considered "a soused gurnet" as low an appellation as he could put his tongue to, and the very name comes from the French *grognard*, or grunter. Thinking men and women are all against it. However, the three fish named come from the Adaja which flows to one side of the city; and it appears too that fish from this river are in the fleshly sense incorruptible, although this is due less to their sanctity as individuals than to the chemical composition of the river bed.

The foregoing has simply been the *amuse-gueule* and the serious part of the meal now looms in front of us. We shall have sucking pig, of course, roasted slowly and lovingly in its own juices to the point where the little body can be sliced with an earthenware plate. After that there should be game, either small like partridge and hare, or large, like boar and mountain goat, for here and in the wild lovely Sierra de Gredos nearby all species are plentiful and of good flavour. From this, go on to a few slices of roast veal, which in Avila is wonderfully white and delicate, in order to give the stomach a rest. Wind up with a thick stew of kid, favourite dish of the regional shepherds, to which the brochure I quote ascribes the military virtues of ancient Avila. And for dessert, there will be *yemas de Santa Teresa*, little round yellow balls, soft as butter and candied as honey, the last thing in the world to put you in mind of the human tornado they are named for; and other local sweet-meats and cakes, as well as the fruit of the countryside and the sweet golden grapes from the "Andalusia of Castile". The meal should be eaten with bread of the fine wheat from La Moraña and washed down by draughts of the heady, delightful Cebreros.

This is all very well, but, as the *yemas* remind us, we are in the birthplace of Teresa de Jesús. It is indeed hard to imagine what she would say to a feast like the one described above. With certain people, of whom Queen Victoria was one, we feel sure we know what they would have said about absolutely anything. We may well be wrong, but the certainty is none the

163

less there. St Teresa is wholly unpredictable and it is one of her countless charms. She might have been Spaniard enough to find pleasure in her city's accomplishment, of however earthy a kind, or woman enough to know the spiritual benefits to struggling humanity of a *bonne boustifaille*. On the other hand, even by Spanish and saintly standards, she was ascetic. We may search her writings in vain for strictures on gluttony or intemperance because, so frugally did she live, they did not even figure in her thoughts. "Oh, go and eat worms!" she once exclaimed, to a novice who came bothering her: whereat, never doubting but that this order was meant literally by one as self-denying as her superior, the poor girl hastened to carry it out, returning only to ask permission to fry them first in a little olive oil.

I do not know how it would be to live the year round in this tiny mediaeval city, self-conscious in having brought forth the greatest Spanish saint and, with St James the Great, Spain's co-patroness; but to visit it is a great experience. The spirit of the place is wholly Teresian, in the sense of fervour and passion side by side with tranquillity. The little public gardens are beautifully kept, the houses are wonderfully clean, the children seem less noisy, the very storks appear to build more carefully and more circumspectly than elsewhere. Outside the massive walls is a wonderful sweep of bare country rolling away as far as the eye can see under the Castilian skies that look somehow higher and wider than those of other places. Inside them are the age-old sights of Spain, the fat old priest reading his breviary, the thin farmer driving his cart, the donkey laden with baskets of long new loaves, the earthenware water jars, the girl carrying her pitcher of milk, the caged birds and caged crickets, the shops full of their rough wooden implements, pitchforks, hayrakes, straw hats as wide as a wheel for the long scorching day in the fields, rope, saddles and harness, all touched with a poetry denied to the gadgets of to-day, all speaking in quiet voices of what Anatole France called "les choses humbles et saintes de la vie". Every May there is a *romería* in honour of Our Lady of the Cows held in front of the oratory of that name, marking the occasion when a farmer left his plough in order to pray to the Virgin and the sagacious beasts carried on and finished the field while he was away. This miracle is familiar in the Latin Christian tradition, and is particularly appreciated in Spain: while here it seems appropriate as well, the most natural thing in the world. And everywhere are charming, rustic or unusual street-names. A narrow lane beside the cathedral is called the *Street of Life and Death* and, although the name only refers to the two *medallones* depicting these subjects on the wall, it need not worry us, whatever the reason, it is the perfect name for a street in Avila.

Everywhere in the city and just beyond its walls are traces or recollections of the saint. Needless to say, her family house became the site of a convent and the little room in which she was born is to-day a tiny airless chapel smothered in gold. In St John's, to one side of the Little Market, is the huge font where she is believed to have been christened. The small graceless church of St Thomas the Elder would hardly be visited at all perhaps, had it not been the scene of a furious attack upon her, made in her presence, by an obscure but fanatical preacher. Her first foundation, the Convento de Las Madres, has a number of homely things of hers, the bench she sat on while writing, the block she used as a pillow, the girdle of her habit, a book by St Gregory with her added notes, a letter, the pitcher she drank from, the flute she played, the nut-tree she planted, the stairway the Devil caused her to fall down on; and her collar-bone. This last is the only trophy of the kind, although the convent housed all her remains for a year or so before their final translation to Alba de Tormes, near Sala-manca: remains being the exact word for them, for such was the fragrance of her dead body that her pious companions madly tore bits off it. Fr Gracian, or Fra Jerome of the Mother of God, the "Eliseus" she referred to so often in the *Relations*, her latter-day confessor and great friend, whom she believed to stand in the place of God beside her and to whom she took a vow of absolute obedience – with, at the same time, certain wonderfully characteristic little afterthoughts and reservations – this same Fr Gracian chopped off one of her hands.

Of all the Teresian sites in Avila the most impressive is the Monasterio de la Encarnación, in which the saint first took the habit in 1533 and of which she was later to become prioress. It lies beyond the city wall on the north side, a plain old building in a simple precinct, cared for by a woman who lives to one side and must be hunted up from her cooking or fowl-keeping to open the doors. Everything here is untouched and unrestored, the wooden pillow, the uneven stone flags of the floor, the beams of the ceiling: all is harsh and bare, and yet mysteriously inhabited. Humble surroundings that have seen the birth of great enterprises have often this feeling about them, as if their very wood and stone were somehow saturated with faith and valour. Near her own little cell, and that in which St John of the Cross heard her confessions, is a third, where she saw St John of the Cross, St Peter of Alcántara, St Luis Beltrán and St Francisco de Borja, one of the few dukes to become a saint, as well as her friends in the world. Here she had her first vision of Christ, and the tormenting manifestations which led to her severing contact with the outside world and devoting herself entirely to the planning of the reformed Discalced Carmelite Order: which led in turn to the journeys over Spain for the recruiting of nuns, every one of whom had to be fit to become a prioress, and the setting up of the sixteen reformed houses, so warmly, merrily and brilliantly described in *The Foundations*.

Ford waves St Teresa aside as "the crazy nun" and waxes wroth at her appointment as a commander of the Spanish forces against the French in the Peninsular War, saying that the place belonged entirely to the Apostle James, who was at least a man. It is pleasant to reflect that an enlightened Victorian

Protestant gentleman of classical education, wide reading and natural genius can be just as nutty as the rest of mankind. The military reputation of St James the Great reposes mainly on his personal appearance and doughty deeds at the battle of Clavijo in the Ebro valley in A.D. 834, when he led the Christians against the Moors and by a most implacable slaughtering earned for himself the name of Santiago Matamoros; but there are scholars, even Spanish ones, who deny not merely that he ever appeared there, which is the kind of nasty thing we expect of scholars, but also that there was any battle at Clavijo at all. The one sure thing about the event is that the Chapter of Santiago's Cathedral at Compostela exacted tribute from the rest of Spain for several centuries in consequence: a most diverting as well as scholarly account of this affair is in T. D. Kendrick's *Saint James in Spain*. Be all that as it may, in a scrap I would rather have St Teresa beside me than fourteen men, apostles or otherwise. As to craziness, one of her great qualities was in fact her splendid and entirely Spanish common-sense, which may sound a dull thing but in the degree she possessed it was luminous and exhilarating and indeed, in times like our own, would be wellnigh magical. But Sir Richard is entitled to his opinion and some may prefer his blunt expression of Victorian prejudice to the pseudo-medical patter with which various contemporary writers have attempted to whittle the saint down to their measure.

But everything ever said by anyone about this wonderful person seems irrelevant, shadowy and without substance when one stands on the floor that she trod and looks out through her arched gateway up to her own city. Having followed the *via teresiana* as usual the day after my arrival, towards evening I strolled out along the Salamanca road and over the Old Bridge. The river was low, with pretty little green islands in it where animals stood and drank, the water catching the pink and yellow tints in the sky. Some way up the hill on the other side were the Cuatro Postes, the little open-air oratory of Grecian aspect that marks the spot where Teresa and her brother, having run away from home as young children to seek martyrdom overseas, were found and taken back by an uncle; and under it now sat a fresh-faced girl of twenty or so in the blue habit and winged cap of St Vincent de Paul, controlling her flock of a hundred or more fiendish little orphan boys by piercing blasts on a tin whistle. Sheep of many kinds scrambled up and down the rocky slopes in the care of a shepherd, whose face might have been carved from mahogany: the plaintive ringing of their bells as they moved was the sweet characteristic sound of the Spanish countryside.

There were plenty of people about, priests with red sashes, courting couples, families, all with the air of gravity and restraint that is so much part of the Castilian temper. There was a tavern by the side of the road, a long white cabin with an enormous vine growing all along it, and great slabs of rock dotted about the grass to serve as chairs. In the garden beside it men of all ages were playing a game, consisting of throwing a heavy bar of stone at a bent arm of wood in the endeavour to break it: they were solemn and absorbed as children, good shots evoking no applause, bad ones no ribaldry. Some of the older ones wore the traditional cummerbund of black and once an old couple trotted by on horseback in full Castilian rig, all black from head to foot, the woman wearing a voluminous belted skirt. From this point the view of Avila was quite superb: in the gentle light of evening the walls round it looked like a loop of velvet ribbon, the colour of honey, ruched here and there where the battlements came.

And far away in the tremendous plain, bravely flying the national flag and dwarfing all else, was yet another great *colegio* for the orphans of Spanish railway-workers.

❧ *15* ❧

BARCELONA CONSIDERS HERSELF MORE FRENCH THAN
Spanish, nearer to Paris than to Madrid. It is her own little
ilusión and how the stranger will feel about it depends of course
on where he has come from. If from Port Bou, he probably
will disagree. From the moment he changes into the broad-
gauged Spanish train with its peculiar rhythm and leisurely
stops, and is trundled away over the vivid red earth and past
campesinos so brown, shrivelled and dusty they seem to have
been raked out of one of their own bonfires, he will be con-
scious of an entirely new "feel" to things which the great city
ahead will not belie. But he may be coming from Castile or
Andalusia, and in that case things will wear a very different
aspect.

I once arrived from Granada, by TAF. It was in March and
the sun was gentle enough still for the other passengers to
allow me to keep a blind up. The whole of the way they slept,
ate or discreetly made love to babies in arms, this being an old
and approved Spanish method of making love to their mothers.
The TAF meanwhile was lurching and rattling through some
of the grimmest country in the whole of Spain. Often for as
far as the eye could see there was not a yard of land growing
anything for human use, nothing but a dead pinkish desert
speckled with ilex and scrub and rock. At every small halt by
the way people came running up to see the train, whose arrival
no doubt was the chief event of the day. The men were burned
nearly black by years of labour under the sun and were dressed
in wide hats, corduroy suits and with a blanket slung as a

cloak. *La espaciosa y triste España*: Fray Luis de Leon's phrase came often to mind as we roared past the dusty yellow hills with their caves and cave-dwellers, the desolation of Elche, the weird mountain ranges, now grey, bizarre and lowering, now green and wrinkled like enormous tents that buckle on the point of collapse; and past the tiny dwellings here and there, separated by such formidable distances, and the tiny human beings labouring in pockets of earth that clung between cliffs in the gorges.

At Valencia, exhausted, I took a plane; and suddenly to come from an experience of that kind to Barcelona, to the animation, the lights, the *muchadumbre*, the motors shrilly hooting as they darted along the crowded boulevards, the streaming fountains, was indeed somewhat like arriving in Paris. And quite a number of things there, great or small, may appear to support the city's idea of itself. There is many a touch of provincial France in the side streets with their shabby cafés and tall grey houses and the high plane trees throwing a green shade over the cobbles. The Underground, moreover, has a noticeably French smell. A music-hall of huge indecency down by the port is supposed to be modelled on the Moulin Rouge, although the indecency is wholly Spanish, being curiously innocent and child-like, and rather engaging. In casual contacts, too, we may come up against that peculiar, invincible disagreeableness that is a noteworthy feature of *la belle France*. If we hail a taxi the driver, hand admirably co-ordinating with brain, sets the meter to work before he even slows down. If we ask for a glass of *coñac* the waiter pours it so diffidently, by dribs and drabs, up to the red line round the *copita*, you'd think one drop too much would entail his instant dismissal, if not arrest. To this there will of course be many exceptions, but I speak of the general climate. To say that the prevailing wind is from the north does not mean that a south wind never blows.

It is very much a going concern, this largest of Mediterranean ports. There are tall factory chimneys with plumes of brown smoke reaching half across the sky. On a foggy day soot curls and wriggles in tadpole fashion through the air, feeling the way to a clean collar or face, catching the throat like a whiff of gas, making the eyes tingle. There are great ships in the harbour, great banks, great warehouses, Chinese restaurants and foreign newspapers by the dozen. The drinking water tastes of disinfectant. And there is a proletariat here, not *pobres* with a place even if humble and wretched in the community, but a *plebs*, raucous, defiant and international.

Barcelona, moreover, looks forward and out, she does not drowse and cackle like an old hen on an empty nest. She busies herself with art and literature, she is willing to experiment and to startle. Driving about the city you will now and again happen on a lunatic building by the "tortured genius" Gaudi, if not on his masterpiece itself, the Church of the Holy Family, its spires thrusting skyward like so many dental drills. Only in Barcelona, they will tell you, could such a thing have been imagined and partly realized. During the Civil War the anarchists very properly tried to burn it down, but the material used in building it would not catch fire. It stands there yet unfinished, hideous and indestructible. Gaudi's tragedy was to be born before his time: he would have been just the man for the Disney Island contract.

But Barcelona has other shots in her locker, besides Gaudi and fog and proles: besides even the human attractions of climate, position and scenery. Alone of Spanish cities, she has that indefinable but thrilling feel of the big city. At Montjuich she has one of the great museums of Europe where the flowering of mediaeval Catalan genius is wonderfully resumed and set forth: a place like the Prado in which to lose oneself for hours and days on end. At Barceloneta there are the fish restaurants. When I recently referred to these noble institutions in talk with a rich American he gave me one of those smiles and remarked that they were very "old hat"; and let us thank God for it, it is probably why we seldom see rich Americans there.

Take a 64 tram through the sooty environs of the harbour works to the terminus, which looks as squalid as can be. Do not be tempted by barrow boys selling *mariscos* and cut lemon on the kerb, for better things still lie ahead. Cross the road, turn up an alley through a little slum, trudge over loose grey sand and bits of old saucepan and newspaper with famished dogs and cats nosing about in it until you come to a row of marquees side by side, like attractions in a fair. Outside each is a shallow round wicker basket the size of a cart-wheel, with crayfish, lobsters, deep sea prawns, bay prawns, spider crabs, sole, mullet, squid, mussels, clams, cockles, artfully laid out on a bed of cracked ice. The kitchen is just inside the tent, and you walk through it, excited as a horse by the hissing and steaming and exotic smelling, to the restaurants, which are right on the beach. Everything is as simple as possible, the cloths and napkins are in rough blue check, the rolls are like small loaves, the bottles have no label, the waiting is of the here-am-I-where-are-you school: organization, externals, are kept to a minimum so we may savour the more fully with single heart and mind the *voluptas* of eating perfectly cooked fish newly out of the sea, with the sound of waves breaking in our ears and the sun dancing on the water before our eyes. To have enjoined the eating of this glorious food on the faithful as a mortification of the flesh is one of the stranger of Mother Church's acts; and did we not know she is always right, we might suspect the Devil himself of having put her up to it. But I am letting myself go.

The Barcelona legend had been so rubbed into me for so long that I never wanted to go there and when I had to I scuttled away at the first opportunity. The precious truth came slowly and painfully, resisted, as so often, every inch of the way. I well remember the first little breach in my defences, made early one morning in June. It was in a café off the Via Layetana, the grimy bustling street of *quehaceres* that runs from the Plaza Cataluña down to the Correos. To my surprise there was only one waiter in it, fast asleep with a transistor bawling into his ear and two days' beard on his chin. No Andalusian could have given a more threatening scowl than he when I woke him up or have slouched away for the order with more dragging steps. When a quarter of an hour had passed and nothing had happened I became, furthermore, aware of a sensation within me, a kind of seething or boiling familiar in Arcos, Baeza or Trujillo, but totally unexpected in French Barcelona. The waiter reappeared, still heavily scowling, and strode purposefully towards me with nothing in his hands but a small piece of wood. Stooping, he carried out one of the great familiar endearing Spanish rituals, namely, the wedging of a table's leg to prevent it from rocking. Then he went away. After ten more minutes he came back with my breakfast, and now he was broadly smiling, the triumphant smile Spain gives her guests when she has been able to make them happy. Being in French Barcelona I had asked for coffee, piping hot and very strong, and a croissant: what I received was a cup of cool grey liquid, a sugared bun and a small jar of apricot syrup. The waiter returned to his chair, cleared his breathing passages with singular emphasis, turned up the radio a little and fell asleep. I had my breakfast, laid the money for it on the table and, with a strange feeling of happy sadness, crept away. Turning for a last look at the café, I observed that its name was *El Dinámico*.

I went down the Ramblas, through the dappled sun and shadow, past the great fiery bursts where roses, carnations, lilies and gladioli are banked on the stalls, thinking for the first time how truly, how exclusively Spanish they were, the people lively but not bustling, animated but not vivacious, the women walking and dressing well, their clothes sombre, their hair dyed in many strange and vivid colours. Trams were whining and clanging up and down under the leafy boughs, police whistled at the traffic like madmen and the air smelled of hot olive oil. There was a man in a beret and white overall saying he had roots and seeds and bulbs, and that nothing sold by him ever failed to come up. His collection looked all right on the whole, candidum, paeony, arum, anemone, but what could those large fawn wrinkled objects be, those over there like withered parsnips? They were labelled – but could hardly be – paeony. The seedsman concurred: the label was displaced and the roots in fact were *claveles*, or carnations. He stuck to that. The proposition was outrageous enough to be interesting. I cross-examined him as to their culture. Put them in the ground, he said, without hesitation. Well in. His conversation had a flavour of *Alice in Wonderland*. When did they flower? Any time. All the year round. But they started – at this he stabbed the air with a lean forefinger to emphasize what he said – they started in mid-winter. Would Ireland be too cold for them? And where was Ireland? Beside England. Ah, just the thing. They don't mind cold. They revel in wet. They love everything. What colour were they? Any colour you fancy. . . . . He smiled as two or three of the roots were bought but the sight of a hundred peseta note destroyed the mood altogether. He ran with it to the flower-woman across the way, a vast creature spilling like risen bread over the side of her corset and with a roman nose and hair in a purple beehive. She shook her head without a word while continuing to stare before her into space. On to the next stall he flitted, and the next, and the next, a lean white figure threading his way through the crowd like Polichinelle. Would he ever come back? He was coming already, and looked more dejected than ever. The resources of the Rambla were at an end: his own particular Rambla, that is to say, for he would not dream of crossing the border into the one higher up. He gently pushed the air before him down with the palms of his hands, as if curbing an exuberant dog, a Spanish gesture meaning Wait, have patience, and he dashed into the nearest bar, and out again, indignantly waving the money. Into a *tabacalera* and out, into a souvenir shop and out. It was absurd and he knew it. In one of the busiest streets of the richest city in Spain no one seemingly could or would change a hundred pesetas. The Iberia office has a poster on the wall showing the globe with Barcelona plumb in the middle and the rest of the world spread all about, which bears the caption: *Barcelona, centro del mundo*. All the same, Barcelona had no change for a hundred pesetas. Polichinelle by now was spinning like a top with shame and anxiety, vexation and heat; and presently he fell so low as to consult a policeman. The *guardia* shrugged and vaguely pointed towards the sea. . . .

Everyone, incidentally, who visits Barcelona should from this day forth spend all the time he can in the Ramblas, as rumour persistently declares they are to be done away with, in the name of better circulation. It is so preposterous that it is all too likely to be true. The trees must come down and the flowers be swept away and the lively shady walks turned into something like the Pasco de Gracia, named, no doubt, after some tiny fat general. The excuse given is the market off to one side, certainly a focus of *animación* with the piles of tomatoes and peppers glowing under the electric light and purple onions as crisp and sweet as apples, the trays of woven rush containing bright Mediterranean fish so beautifully fresh and cold that flies will never go near them, the alarming joints of meat and the little bars all dark and small, tucked away in corners where the merchant may slip in for a hurried go of anis or brandy. But this is a mere pretext, we suspect: the true reason is more likely to be the frenzy for construction at any price and of any sort that has Spain in its lethal grip, for the clawing out of the hearts of cities and the filling in of the cavities with rubbish of the Franco-Franco-Franco school.

The little to-do with the seedsman reminded me that money from home should by now have arrived in one of the local banks, and thither I next turned my steps. There is no better place than a bank in which to study a national temper. The important ones of Barcelona are nearly all in or near the Plaza Cataluña and it was here that the banking force of the city held its famous demonstration against the one-hour-for-lunch rule: elsewhere in Spain it caused consternation, even despair, without giving rise to action. The *plaza* on that occasion was black with banking men, managers and doormen alike, aggrieved but still perfect gentlemen, strolling up and down with their frugal *bocadillos* and their austere drinks of water. Thither I now went to the bank in question and inquired for my draft, thereby setting off a train of events which I will describe because as far as I was concerned it settled the matter of Barcelona's nationality once and for ever, to my entire satisfaction and lasting happiness.

A magnificent man in uniform of military cut received clients in a towering marble hall and sorted them out. He led the way through other echoing halls to where a number of worried youths in their shirtsleeves were nestling together like rabbits in a hutch. One of these came forward and hearing the facts of my case from the lips of the majordomo regretted at once that nothing had so far come and requested that I should call again some other day. He was so positive that I did not dare ask him to make sure; and so I did as he bade me, having in the interval telegraphed to my own bank and received reply that the draft had been sent over ten days ago.

The young man was there again and made the same reply but this time with a frown of vexation and his colleagues likewise looked sulkily away. It was a nice state of affairs, they seemed to be thinking, when busy men could not proceed with their business without a plague of foreigners descending on them with nonsensical inquiries and unfounded assertions. I waved the telegram from home at the youth and he became really put out. Did I seriously imagine a bank would withold money once it was there? It was not: one had to have patience in dealing with foreign matters. Let the Señora come again tomorrow, but later, later: let her leave it as late in the day as she could. This I did, and was prepared to be a little rough myself, only to be met with beaming smiles from the entire section. Excitedly, their ringleader flourished a letter from my own bank on which I could not but perceive the date-stamp of his, a week old. There followed another familiar and deeply satisfying Spanish ritual, as he collected my passport and with two fingers slowly typed out a form in triplicate: showing the result to a colleague, for two heads are better than one, and then to another, for three are better still: finally calling in a consultant from a different department altogether and holding with him a long bubbling conversation, or rather duet, for neither paused to hear the other out; and signalling to me next to depart with the majordomo for a strange and faraway place and wait there till he himself headed an expedition to the vaults to learn if that much money were contained in them. At last the notes were in my hand and, with everyone still broadly smiling, for Spain had risen to the occasion and proved herself second to none in the management of intricate financial affairs, I passed from the lofty marble halls to the clear hot sunshine and sank, weary and dry, on to a chair in what seemed to be an open-air café. It turned out to be the Circle for Army Officers and Their Families, but no matter, I was served all the same. I have remarked before on the very courteous and civilized habit of Spanish clubs in serving complete strangers in this way. My friend Jaime says it is merely because they are perennially hard-up; but the day I wring a good word for Spain from Jaime the sky will undoubtedly fall in.

And so there I sat in Spanish Barcelona, with no wish to be anywhere else. I called out to the waiter to bring me the bill, but he was wedging a table to stop it rocking and made as if he did not hear. A Spaniard cannot or will not allow two things into his head at a time. We must never ask him what's o'clock if he is reading the paper or the way to somewhere if he is fastening a bootlace. He will not give a surly dismissive Gallic shrug if we do but will go steadily on with what he is doing as if we had never spoken. To be treated in this fashion is to experience loneliness. But while his mind rejects a second and alien theme as an intolerable interruption, he can follow and mentally participate in an extraordinary range of activities going on round him when he likes. Women are particularly keen practitioners of this art; it is my good luck to know one of the keenest of them all. A tiny placid woman with a brown face and a mane of silver hair, she will sit surrounded by, say, three of her children and their spouses and eleven, or nineteen, of her grandchildren, taking the lead in whatever family conference may be in progress and at the same time fluently admonishing encouraging or soothing the *angelitos*. Apart from this, she is bound to be telephoning to one of her tradesmen. She has a rubber claw fitted to the receiver, so that it nestles on her shoulder and against her ear like a parrot and need not hinder her sewing, ironing, making her accounts up or sipping Fundador. Simultaneously with the family conference and the children and the telephone she will follow with keen enjoyment the *flamenco* hour on the wireless. Into all this the maid may well come bounding with the news that the water has been turned off all over the block whereat, with a cry of *¡Qué raro!* my friend gives instructions about it, her voice riding the *tohubohu* as effortlessly as any prima donna's a chorus.

Now the waiter had finished putting in the wedge and I called to him again. With a cheery cry of *"En seguida!"* he disappeared for a quarter of an hour.

At last I got away and strolled up the Paseo de Gracia, thinking a quiet visit to the cool airs above the city would attractively round off the afternoon. The shops and offices were beginning to empty out and the crowds of hurrying bodies seemed to send the temperature up. A battered old tram waited in the little square above, with a few Spaniards and one foreign tourist in it. He had a most intelligent face and long yellow hair, and there were thick rims to his spectacles. He looked pleased with himself, I noted: perhaps he was trying to "get the feel of the country" by travelling in the public conveyances and friends had warned him that these are apt to be crowded, so that he felt pardonably one up. There is something infinitely touching about a look of that sort on a foreign face in Spain. A sharp blow on a bell announced imminent departure: this particular tram has to be punctual because it goes only half way up the Tibidabo and connects with a funicular that completes the ascent. The blond tourist looked at his watch and smiled in approval but instead of gliding smoothly forward the tram remained at rest. And as if by magic a crowd sprang up and hurled itself at it: every seat had gone in a twinkling, seized by the younger stronger men, after which their seniors and the infirm, women and children, poured in to fill the aisles and the space between the seats and after that the platforms outside and finally the very steps. Everywhere human beings clung to whatever they found, like bats in a cave. The Spaniards were shouting in high good humour but the glow was gone from the tourist's eye, for a stout child sat upon his knee and blew gum bubbles into his face and half a dozen chickens balanced in a straw container on his head. Groaning, the tram collected its powers together and began creeping over the ground: if that is how it managed on the flat what was to become of it round the corner where the hill began? Nothing much, except that the groans were louder and the pace slower, slower and slower until positively the vehicle inched its way along and the sulks of the tourist gave way to intense alarm. At last it ground to a halt, twenty minutes after the funicular was due to leave, and peering from beneath his unusual head-dress he saw that we were merely at the first stop and that a small new army was preparing to storm its way on board. The dejected slump of his shoulders made it clear that his interest in the feel of the country had subsided.

A swarm of Spaniards can melt as rapidly as it collects, however, and this one had vanished within a minute of arriving at the base of the funicular. It was difficult to imagine where all those bodies had got to unless, as seemed unlikely, they had flocked into the Home for Dogs nearby. The Englishman and I each had a half of the funicular for our own, but now his spirit was gone. At every pause up the mountainside his head came out of a window like the head of an apprehensive turtle, turning this way and that, this way and that.

From the top of Tibidabo on a fine summer evening Barcelona looks enchanting, the seas round her grimy shore a dark violet and her pine-covered hills swimming in huge baths of yellow light, the business-men's villas scattered about them glowing each with its own private halo. It is important, however, to disregard the horrid sights about us, for enterprise has reared its head up here as well. A Salesian church of repellent aspect crowns the peak itself and, to commemorate the temptation in the wilderness, the Societa Anónima Tibidabo provides scenic railways, aerial flights, telescopes, gocars, souvenirs and, needless to say, Coca-Cola, as well as a section specified, somewhat oddly in view of all the rest, as *atracciones infantiles*. It is as if a simple shepherd lad, watching his flocks on the lonely mountainside, had had a sudden overpowering vision of Blackpool or Luna Park and vowed never to rest until he had established something of that order in Cataluña's green and pleasant land. But alas, all the things Barcelona plumes herself on, from fun fairs to factories, are to be had much better elsewhere. She and her people grow on us in the measure that we can work through the shopfront and come on what lies behind, despite all endeavours to head us off. It is a matter of grief, this, to the Catalan lost in his dreams of skyscrapers and bustle and Latin-American chic, of progress and efficiency; and may perhaps account a little for his somewhat crusty ways.

❧ *16* ❧

THERE IS NOTHING FRENCH ABOUT LA SEU, AT ALL events. This is the oldest Gothic cathedral in all Cataluña and surely it must be the darkest in all Spain, a huge black pit with here and there a blaze of candlelight, a small red eye of lamp or glint of gold from statue. In many Gothic cathedrals the soaring effect of the exterior is somehow repeated or suggested inside, here all seems to crouch and cower. Nothing could ever take wing in it, you feel, the gold and the jewels weigh too heavy. The organist and the choir are as completely at odds as anywhere else and the crowds of the faithful are as Spanish as can be, with the stout old ladies in black expressing their disapproval of foreign clothing and demeanour by a vigorous non-stop movement of the fan, the children playing their secret little games, the *señoritos* daintily spreading a handkerchief on the ground before they kneel, the old men standing bolt upright with an air of not really being there at all and the peasant women in their wide skirts and shawls and kerchiefs kissing the hands and feet of their own particular saint. Among them we see over and over again the Catalan face, every bit as distinctive in its way as the Castilian, long with a curved new-moon sort of length rather than the straight, bony-old-ram's length of Castile: upward curved chin, upward curved nose with a pointed tip, something a little foxy about the whole effect as with Our Lady of Montserrat or some of the figures in mediaeval Catalan painting: the colouring of these people is often blond or reddish, never washed-out or anaemic.

On festive nights the spires, façades and precincts are floodlit in a lovely expanse of honey-coloured stone with iridescent patches of ruby, sapphire, emerald and rose where stained-glass windows occur: at such times the whole great building seems ardently to glow from within. Round the corner Ramon Berenguer III, Count of Barcelona, founder of ancient Catalan sea-power, rides his mount on the ivy-covered pedestal, a small romantic figure from the twelfth century in a pool of modern light. Behind him is a little sunk garden with flower-beds and trees and stone benches and, leaping from the shadow of the ruins behind, an odd white statue in flowing draperies, one of the innumerable headless classical statues of Spain that make one think of an army of Visigothic housemaids charging over the face of the land in Hunnish fury. All round are the little streets of old Barcelona with the pear-drop lamps surmounted by their sooty crowns and the tiny shops open to all hours, the taverns and eating-houses blowing puffs of vinous, oily, garlicky breath through door and window and the alleyways where string upon string of multi-coloured washing hangs to dry, like the flags of a triumphant army.

The cloisters of the cathedral and the twisting lanes nearby have a flavour all their own and would make a splendid background for a film, a truthful rather than an edifying one perhaps, for the plump black figures bustling to and fro have an air that is anything but spiritual. I am particularly fond of the Calle de Paradís running up past the cathedral to the Plaza de San Jaime which, containing both the Town Hall and the Diputación, is the finest square of the city. In this little street are the remains of a Greek temple to Augustus Caesar, some wall engravings commemorating brave gentlemen of Barcelona shot by the French and a shop which appeals by its very absurdity, as everything in it is made of wax. Besides the expected candles of every size and shape for burning at shrines there is a fantastic medley of fruit, birds, fish, saints and even *banderillas*: it is not easy to think why anyone should take a real *banderilla* home, and why a wax one is past all imagining. Another endearing feature of this enterprise is that the moment the sun is up the blinds must come down lest the stock melt away altogether: so that for the greater part of the day we must be content with a faint mawkish smell coming through the door.

Coming down this little street one evening I found San Jaime floodlit, the balconies of the buildings gay with aprons, His Excellency the Governor leaning over the biggest of them and the whole square crammed with rings of people dancing *sardanas*. In the middle was a platform on which sat the band, blowing and banging in a methodical, curiously Germanic way. The *sardanas* themselves, grave beautiful tests of endurance, were hypnotic in their cumulative effect as on and on they went, the white-clad dancers holding up each other's hands in the stern, comfortless way, men and women supporting each other, carrying grimly on, feet deliberately and solemnly treading the measure to the plaintive cry of *fabiol* and *tenora*, faces wooden, on and on and on until at last they all exploded in frenzied leapings. The youths and girls in white with belts of green, blue, scarlet or mauve were dancing in competition, but all over the square others were spontaneously joining in, boys and girls, children, middle-aged men and ladies old enough and stout enough, one would have said, to think twice about it but bravely puffing and panting away to beat the band.

Poorly executed *flamenco* is ludicrous, *sardanas* are never less than compelling. They should not be seen in a theatre where one cannot give oneself up to their lugubrious spell, but always in the open streets where the monotony and repetition are an added charm. The Catalan gravity is different from the Andalusian and Castilian: it is dogged, not intense, plebeian and not aristocratic, and it has a charming gaucherie. One of the loveliest and most moving of all Spanish folk dances is the

Catalan sequence of Sant Vicens, portraying the passion, death, burial and resurrection of Christ, carried out by boys and girls in white clothes or the dress of the region. Except for their long torches they dance in darkness, going through a few quiet movements to waves of the lighted torch and then freeze in a tableau, Christ tied to the pillar, on the Cross, dead in the Virgin's arms, in the grave and finally risen. All taking part have an air of despondency: they do not acknowledge applause. While they feel very much the force of what they represent, they do not give any sign of smugness or piousness or, indeed, of any emotion at all: there is just the strange wooden gravity and child-like concentration, the naïvety, the clumsiness, all infinitely appealing.

On and on, on and on: a beautiful square beautifully lit, full of dancing bodies and not one smiling face. With the haunting notes of the music, playing always the same tune, it became a little weird. At half-past one the band quietly packed its instruments and everybody walked away without a word. After High Mass next morning the whole thing was re-enacted at the foot of the cathedral steps, in blazing sunshine now but with the same unshakeable gloom of demeanour.

That afternoon the same stolid people were massed in their thousands at the Monumental to see El Viti and two other heroes. I sat behind a little bunch of connoisseurs collected under an umbrella of cigar smoke just above the heads of the managers and impresarios and hangers-on. The experts were brown and fat, with diamonds sparkling on their fingers and paunches that shook and leaped and tumbled with emotion. Out there on the sand El Viti was tranquil, composed, almost unmoving, so completely in charge that his bull seemed to gambol about him like a large and friendly dog. The connoisseurs approved, even the professional critic who looked as sour as a green lemon and was making notes on the back of a paper bag. All of them knew all the others and they continually shouted to each other in rich bubbling voices. A great fighter!

Timing, dominion, the lot! Perfection! But El Viti muffed the kill. Instantly the great voices poured out a stream of advice and disparagement. Not one of them would have lasted five seconds in the job, but they were all ablaze with scorn. At last the bull was despatched and they rallied at once to El Viti again because he was awarded only one ear. They roared and whistled up at the President in company with twenty thousand others, for the Spaniard who could not run the *corrida* better than the man who is actually doing it has yet to be born. The President was unmoved among the gold and crimson trappings of his box. "Fool!" shrieked the crowd in his direction. "Wretch! Incompetent!" They whistled away like a yardful of locomotives. But one ear it was, and El Viti marched round the ring holding it up amid a shower of hats and flowers and purses and other small objects, all of which, except the flowers, were thrown back. While the horses dragged the bull away and workmen ran about freshening the sand the connoisseurs bubbled over in rapid gossip about the bull to come, of a famous Sevillan breed and the heaviest by far of the whole afternoon. The sweet thrilling note of the *clarín* sounded, the gates were flung back and the bull roared in: verily his neck was clothed with thunder, he seemed to shake the arena with his mighty hooves, no one was in any hurry at all to engage him. When the turn of the *picador* came, with one toss of his wonderful head he sent both man and mount ingloriously sprawling on the sand. At this the passion of the crowd became tinged with a deep mystical fervour and they struck up a litany of praise. *Toro maravilloso! toro precioso!* Bang! the second *picador* had gone the way of the first. *O toro de toros! toro glorioso, estupendo, incomparable!* The connoisseurs had leaped up and were embracing each other. But very soon the joy of the worshipping pack turned to fury again for the *espada* was off his stroke, he did nothing right and indeed very little wrong, he would not hazard his frame within the sweep of those horns. The bull ran gaily about the ring at his own sweet will as if he were alone in it. Coward! screamed the pack. Bungler! *Fuera fuera fuera!* The connoisseurs flailed the air with their podgy fists, they whistled and hooted and booed: the noise must have been clearly heard on the African coast.

I could not stay to the end because Jaime had invited me to visit San Cugat; and I forbore to raise the matter of Catalan morgue in the dance and Catalan ebullience in the ring because he is implacably anti-bullfight, not because he thinks it cruel or primitive but because it is Spanish. He is also implacably anti-clerical, anti-government and anti-Spain-altogether: in a word, he himself is Spanish to the core. Like many of his countrymen he must have two jobs in order to keep alive and he writes articles and advertisements in the evening. Soon after he moved into the flat he now occupies he was disturbed while trying to think by resounding blows from a hammer in the flat next door. He put up with this for a week or so and then went round to inquire. They told him they were having the place done up by a man who could not come in the day-time as he worked in an office. While they were arguing the man from the flat on the other side came round as well. He was trying to sleep, he complained, and this was the only time he could do so: as well as teaching in a school all day he was night watchman in a factory from midnight to seven a.m. How could he fairly divide his forces between the youth of Spain and the interests of the factory-owner if he never closed an eye? It is against an endless tangle of inconvenience, makeshift and privation that all Spanish attitudes have to be considered; and I would not in the least blame Jaime if he were anti absolutely everything.

He was waiting at the railway station in Cataluña now, polite and gloomy as ever. I had proposed an outing to Montserrat, but that had been really too much. The only religious foundations he could endure were those in the latter stages of decrepitude: going concerns he could not abide. He was particularly severe with the Fathers of Montserrat for charging so much and being so businesslike. Certainly, the place is not cheap: the hostel and the restaurant charge rather more than one of the Government *paradores*. The standard of everything is at least as good, however, and one should reflect that it is visited every year by crowds of people, other than the faithful, who merely want to see the mountain, and also that every bite and sup must be dragged up from far away below. A few days up here is one of the great experiences that Spain offers. There is a wonderful happy peace about it all, with quiet walks about the flowery sweet-scented mountainside and enormous views across fantastic country, not to speak of the good cold mountain air. The choir of the music school is relayed to all the public rooms, so that one is never long without the heavenly sound of boy-soprano voices. Conforming to Benedictine tradition, the place is most efficiently run: everything is there, everything works, everything has been thought out and seen to, all without fuss or bother or apparent effort. I can never go up too often, or grudge a single peseta spent; but Jaime wags his puritanical young head and croaks something about the vow of poverty. No doubt he believes the Fathers should allow us all to descend on them like a plague of locusts and eat ourselves to a standstill for nothing.

He cheered up a little in the train because the gentle green slopes and woods along the way made him think of Surrey, particularly as it had come on to rain. It fairly teemed down, making orange pools all over the orange earth and then, in the Catalan way, left off as suddenly as it had begun. The ancient romanesque monastery, which some think to have been founded by Charlemagne, was the same as ever, slumbering its life away in the sun, consenting to its doom. Raindrops sparkled on the trees outside it like a tangle of sequins; in the shaggy green garden within the cloisters acanthus were everywhere in flower, smoky blue spikes rising superbly from classic leaf. The columns of the cloisters themselves were of a rosy-yellow stone with curious or beautiful themes carved on pedestal or capital.

The old priest who had rescued the monastery from total ruin after the Civil War was still there, and showed us round, his head shaking under the clerical beaver like that of a clockwork toy. He was of the type of enthusiast we frequently come on in this country of indifference and apathy. Slowly and painfully he went from shelf to shelf in the library, taking one precious work down after another in his tremulous old hands and exclaiming "Now just look here!" or "Read this!" as if everyone must be as erudite as himself. "Such things as these," he commented wryly more than once, "are of no interest to the *futbolistas*." Footballers, apparently, were a species he looked on with peculiar abhorrence. He lived in the house adjoining the church, with a Spanish cook and a German archivist. The rooms of it were remarkable, being plainly and sparsely furnished in the Spanish way but each one having some magnificent piece of furniture or painting, with heavily carved doors to them all: and in one was a truly regal four-poster bed, reserved no doubt for the Bishop, with virgins and every conceivable holiness cavorting all over the head-rest.

With a last rueful allusion to the degenerate tastes of the day, the priest said goodbye to us and put out his hand. Jaime seized and kissed it with unction: and we left the old man smiling and nodding after us under the massive arch of the monastery gate, one of the resigned devoted old custodians of dusty old ruins all over the land of Spain. I praised him for his zeal in saving the foundation, and the townspeople who had helped with money, material and labour: and Jaime at once declared that he would have had them all shot if they had dared demur.

This was my last day in Barcelona for a while: it had been a thoroughly Spanish one, what with both High Mass and the bull-fight starting fifteen minutes late, these being the two single things that experts declare always start on time. And later on that evening, as Jaime and I sat in a café, the lights all went out and only the lamps of the motor-cars were left to dart about in the pitch blackness like fireflies. A shuddering moan rose from the throng on the pavement: the waiters rushed out from the café and with the deft movements born of long practice set a candle on each of the tables. And as soon as the emergency arrangements were smoothly working, the lights went on in the great tradition: and, to crown my happiness, the unearthly scream of the fire-engines rose above the other enchanting noises of city and harbour.